14-120-1832

A GENERAL PATTERN FOR
AMERICAN PUBLIC HIGHER EDUCATION

THE CARNEGIE SERIES IN AMERICAN EDUCATION

The books in this series have resulted from studies supported by grants of the Carnegie Corporation of New York, and are published by McGraw-Hill in recognition of their importance to the future of American education.

The Corporation, a philanthropic foundation established in 1911 by Andrew Carnegie for the advancement and diffusion of knowledge and understanding, has a continuing interest in the improvement of American education. It financed the studies in this series to provide facts and recommendations which would be useful to all those who make or influence the decisions which shape American educational policies and institutions.

The statements made and views expressed in these books are solely the responsibility of the authors.

Books Published

Berelson · Graduate Education in the United States
Clark · The Open Door College: A Case Study
Cleveland · The Overseas American
Conant · The American High School Today
Corson · Governance of Colleges and Universities
Glenny · Autonomy of Public Colleges
Henninger · The Technical Institute in America
McConnell · A General Pattern for American Public Higher Education
Medsker · The Junior College: Progress and Prospect
Perkins and Snell · The Education of Historians in the United States
Pierson · The Education of American Businessmen
Thomas · The Search for a Common Learning

A GENERAL PATTERN

FOR AMERICAN PUBLIC

HIGHER EDUCATION

T. R. McCONNELL

Chairman of the Center for
the Study of Higher Education,
University of California, Berkeley

McGRAW-HILL BOOK COMPANY, INC.   1962

New York   *San Francisco*   *Toronto*   *London*

A GENERAL PATTERN FOR AMERICAN PUBLIC HIGHER EDUCATION

PREFACE

Some time ago, the Center for the Study of Higher Education of the University of California at Berkeley announced a broad program of studies on the diversification of American higher education.[1] This subject covers such an enormous terrain that it has been necessary to deal with selected parts of it intensively rather than to investigate it comprehensively.

The Center's studies of diversity have been concentrating on three topics: (1) the student body of American higher education, with emphasis on diversity of student characteristics—among and within colleges and universities—in general scholastic aptitude, attitudes, values, and intellectual dispositions or styles; (2) the junior college as a great sorting-out and distributive agency, as well as a means of widening educational opportunity and of absorbing much of the shock of the impending deluge of students; and (3) the state-wide coordination of public higher education.

The Center has undertaken its investigations without a distinct

[1] T. R. McConnell, "The Diversification of American Higher Education: A Research Program," *Educational Record*, vol. 38, pp. 1–16, October, 1957.

practical reference. It has been interested simply in attaining a better understanding of the functioning of American higher education, which has so little uniformity and rationality, and so much diversity in students, organization, control, and output. Nevertheless, the Center's studies do have a definite bearing on one subject of intense current interest and controversy, namely, the pattern of institutions through which a state may provide for the higher education of its heterogeneous student population and for the diverse demands which the American people make on their colleges and universities. The purpose of this volume is to explore the implications of the Center's researches for the patterning of American public higher institutions. Although reference is made to sources other than the Center's studies and reports, there is no attempt to review all the pertinent literature.

Those familiar with American higher education, the subtle nature of human motivation, and the social forces that play on individuals and institutions will not be surprised with the conclusion in the final chapter that no neat pattern can be designed, despite the need for greater rationality and purposeful differentiation. This inability to systematize higher education thoroughly will annoy the doctrinaire in planning and in public administration who is preoccupied with formal structure, stable and tidy organization, and detailed control; and it will baffle the thoughtful educator who would like to make higher education more orderly without organizing it rigidly, or who would like to see students and institutions more effectively paired without infringing unnecessarily on the free choice of either.

Admittedly, an arrangement of institutions into an orderly pattern does not solve the fundamental educational problem, which is to give vitality to educational programs everywhere. But vitality largely depends on a sensible division of responsibilities, on clearly defined institutional functions, on willingness to concentrate on pertinent educational programs, and on appropriate relationships among the institutions comprising an educational system.

Although the educational process is not the subject of this volume, it is of deep interest to the Center for the Study of Higher Education. The Center is engaged in a six-year study of student development in eight diverse institutions varying in size and complexity of organization. The study encompasses the characteristics of the student bodies and of the institutions, and the way in which the institutions exert their influence—if they have a significant impact—on their students. The Center is also studying changes during a four-year period in a group of exceptional students—some nine hundred winners of National Merit Scholarship Corporation awards. Reports of these investigations will appear in due course.

Perhaps a word should be said here about the reason for omitting a discussion of the role of private institutions in a comprehensive, state-wide program of higher education. The writer strongly believes in the value of the American dual system of private and public support and control of colleges and universities. It is obvious that the full resources of both groups of institutions will have to be used if we are to meet the coming demand for higher education. This means that the relationships of public and private institutions will become increasingly important.

It is apparent, also, that the future provision of public higher education, and the relationships of the public and private sectors, will depend in considerable part on the traditional balance between public and private higher education from state to state. Planning the development of higher education in California, where the enrollment is predominantly in public institutions, presents somewhat different problems from those in New York, where private colleges and universities have played the dominant role in enrollment and influence. Yet the balance in New York is changing. It has been predicted that the present division of enrollment, 40 per cent in public and 60 per cent in private institutions, will be reversed in the next decade. As public higher education in New York expands, its relationships with the private sector will not diminish in importance, but, as the text points out, the problems of internal coordination among the institutions comprising the State University of New York will become more complicated, and will increasingly resemble the problems of coordination in states with more highly developed public systems.

For the reasons that public higher education will have to bear the brunt of expanding enrollment, that new public institutions —especially community colleges—will be established in many states, and that questions concerning institutional role may become acute in many places, it was decided to limit this volume to a discussion of the structure of comprehensive, state-wide systems of public colleges and universities.

The systematic development of public higher education involves many problems of educational finance. These problems, important and difficult as they are, are not treated here because they are not being studied by the Center for the Study of Higher Education but are the subjects of extensive investigation and publication elsewhere.

I am indebted, not only to the members of the staff to whose work I have specifically referred in this book, but to many unnamed persons at the Center—consultants, research assistants, and clerical and secretarial personnel. It is a pleasure to acknowledge the editorial assistance of Mr. Max Knight of the University of California Press. Miss Pauline Hunter and Mrs. Marjorie Stultz assisted in the final preparation of the manuscript. I am especially indebted to the Carnegie Corporation of New York, which supported the Center's research on diversity in American higher education. I am grateful for the privilege of spending a year as a fellow at the Center for Advanced Study in the Behavioral Sciences, where the first draft of the manuscript was written.

Various sections of the book have appeared in the following publications, and are used here with permission: *The Educational Record; College and University; The Changing University*, a Report on the Seventh Annual Leadership Conference of the Center for the Study of Liberal Education for Adults (edited by G. H. Daigneault), Chicago, May, 1959; and *The Coming Crisis in the Selection of Students for College Entrance*, American Educational Research Association, Washington, 1960.

T. R. McConnell

CONTENTS

A GENERAL PATTERN FOR
AMERICAN PUBLIC HIGHER EDUCATION

I INTRODUCTION

American colleges and universities have been warned for some time to get ready for a "rising tide" of students. Now it appears that these institutions may be inundated. The U.S. Office of Education recently predicted that 44 per cent of the young people between the ages of eighteen and twenty-four would attend college at some point in the 1960s. But another survey indicates that, arresting as this prediction is, it may be much too low. A broad-based survey conducted for the Ford Foundation in the spring of 1959 by Elmo Roper and Associates showed that 69 per cent of the children below the age of eighteen are expected by their parents to go to college. This would mean almost a tripling of present enrollment—to a college population of 11 million. This startling figure, an officer of the Foundation declared, "demonstrates that a college education has come to be widely regarded as *sine qua non* of personal success, just as the high school diploma did earlier." [1] The same writer then asked what the colleges might do. He offered three alternatives: expand facilities, raise

[1] Elmo Roper and Associates, *The Public Pulse*, no. 6, September, 1959.

standards as a means of restricting admissions, and do both. Actually, all three processes are already under way. It seems obvious, however, that on the present scale, of either action or planning, the expansion of facilities (which must include not only plant but also teachers) will fall considerably short of meeting the needs if only 45 or 50 per cent, rather than 69 per cent, of the age group bang on college doors. Besides, it is doubtful that American higher education will be able to raise standards of admission enough to close the gap between facilities and students.

Faced with the almost insurmountable task of finding money, buildings, equipment, and faculty, it is understandable that institutions are preoccupied with the task of just providing enough places for the horde to come. But the main question is not how to provide enough room somewhere. It is *who* will go to college *where* and *for what?* This is a question American higher education has never frankly faced. Colleges and universities have hidden their own problems and deficiencies behind a barrage of criticism of the high schools. But their own sins are catching up with them, and the day of reckoning is at hand. The demand for post-high-school training by American youths and their parents, which will produce an enrollment of at least 7 million if not 11 million by 1970, together with mounting demands on the public and private purses, will force some hard decisions concerning the broad pattern of American higher education. This is the subject of this book.

Historically, colleges and universities, both public and private, have developed independently and autonomously in this country. The product of this highly decentralized and uncoordinated development is a congeries of institutions varying greatly in government, size, organization, atmosphere, educational program, faculty quality, student characteristics, and intellectual standards. An American university president observed recently that "the outstanding characteristic of the American system of higher education is that it is not a system at all. There is no common pattern of curriculum, instructional method, or organization among our 1,300 degree-granting schools, colleges, and universities." [2]

Much of the present diversity has not been systematically devised but is unplanned and fortuitous. This will always be true to a considerable degree, because in the United States the responsibility for higher education is widely dispersed and divided between the public and private domains. Yet the pressure of numbers and the necessity of securing a vast increase, not only in the absolute amount expended on education beyond the high school but also in the proportion of public revenues reserved for it, will force greater rationalization in the total pattern of American higher education.

In all parts of the country, public higher institutions are under pressure to devise "master plans" for future development, rational and efficient schemes for meeting mounting enrollments. In some instances, this pressure, which ordinarily stems from legislative or executive governmental agencies, is little more than an effort to plot the expansion of existing institutions at minimum cost and with little alteration of their character and functions. In other instances, it is a more imaginative attempt to determine not only the number of students to be served but the kinds of education that will meet their needs most effectively, and to devise a pattern of institutions designed to provide a wide range of educational opportunities economically and with high quality. Thus, the executive director of the Kansas City Association of Trusts and Foundations, Mr. Homer C. Wadsworth, said in a recent commencement address at the University of Missouri that a commission empowered by the Legislature to coordinate the

[2] J. D. Millett, "Colleges Must and Can Be More Efficient," *Planning College Policy for the Critical Decades Ahead*, College Entrance Examination Board, New York, 1958, pp. 50–59.

total program of public higher education in Missouri and to budget funds according to a *"master plan that assigns special functions to each of its parts"* was essential.

Typical of the legislative mandates to planning bodies is the assignment given to the Illinois Commission of Higher Education. The Legislature first directed the commission, composed entirely of lay members, to analyze the future needs for higher education in the state and to study the purposes, types, and programs of institutions that will be required at all levels beyond the high school. At its next session, the Legislature gave the commission the additional assignment "to recommend to the General Assembly, not later than April 1, 1961, a plan for the unified administration of all the State-controlled institutions of higher education."

The situation in Illinois is symptomatic of the problems that other states face. What was once a teachers college under a single governing board for all the teachers colleges has become the University of Southern Illinois with its own board of trustees. The institution is expanding aggressively in its part of the state and has begun to offer doctoral programs. The other state teachers colleges have become universities in name if not in character, although they remain under the control of a single board. One of them, however, encouraged by the success of the University of Southern Illinois, attempted in the 1959 Legislature to secure its own independent governing board. The Commission of Higher Education recommended, however, that the structure and number of governing boards be retained until a complete study could be made of the governmental control of public higher education in Illinois. No doubt in considerable part because of this recommendation, the institution failed to secure a separate governing board, but unless a comprehensive state-wide plan is devised, it might succeed in becoming independent in some future session.

The University of Illinois is about to build a four-year campus in Chicago, where it now has a two-year branch. Unless a constructive plan for the orderly development, government, and coordination of public higher education in the state is adopted, it is not difficult to envision a "separatist movement" as the Chicago section of the university develops, culminating, perhaps, in an independent governing board and in the separation of the present Chicago professional schools from the parent institution at Urbana and their incorporation in the new university.

These are but a few of the variables the Commission of Higher Education had to conjure with in carrying out its mandate to devise a grand design for higher education in Illinois and to coordinate the roles and programs of the constituent institutions in the system.[3] The conditions which produced the complex problems which the commission was created to solve fit neatly into the pattern described in a recent study of state-wide coordination of higher education: [4]

> In addition to the recent large increase in the number of college-age youth and the rate of college attendance, the increasing urbanization during and after World War II has been an added impetus to the establishment of central agencies of coordination. In many states, such as Georgia, Indiana, Ohio, Oregon, Texas, and Wisconsin, the original state universities as well as most of the colleges were located in small towns or lesser cities at some distance from the major cities. Some of these cities as well as certain of the newly developed urban areas have recently succeeded in obtaining a branch of the university, a two-year extension center, or a junior college to help meet their immediate needs. But these facilities are sometimes as poorly planned as to location as the original institutions which they supplement. The populations in these

[3] The proposals of the commission for coordinating higher education in the state will be discussed later.

[4] L. A. Glenny, *Autonomy of Public Colleges: The Challenge of Coordination*, McGraw-Hill Book Company, Inc., New York, 1959, pp. 14–15.

urban centers press for educational opportunities which equal those provided by the older institutions in the rural areas; they want a program of university scope, available at low cost and within commuting distance. Meanwhile existing colleges and universities, both public and private, tend to oppose the establishment of new institutions unless they are able to exert some control and prevent "unfair competition." Thus the problems of financing and planning higher education are compounded both for the legislatures and the institutions.

The necessity for general planning has reached the point where unilateral action is inexcusable. An institution of integrity will make decisions concerning its future with full reference to a larger pattern of responsibility and opportunity. "State by state," said Dr. James Bryant Conant some time ago, "citizens must reappraise the publicly supported educational system from top to bottom and decide what adjustment must be made to handle the vast increase in the numbers of the youth." [5] Even state-wide planning may be insufficient to meet educational needs with the resources available to higher education. Regional planning has proved to be fruitful, as witness the accomplishments of the Southern Regional Education Board and the Western Interstate Commission on Higher Education. In some educational enterprises, nation-wide patterning and support are probably essential. Good examples are the foreign-language and area studies. First the foundations supported these programs in selected universities, and now the Federal government is contributing funds for their expansion and for the creation of new ones. In this instance, the Office of Education is the "coordinating agency."

Planning must be based on assumptions about the future student body. Will higher education react to the mounting number

[5] J. B. Conant, *The Citadel of Learning,* Yale University Press, New Haven, Conn., 1956, p. 77.

of applicants by raising standards of admission, thus excluding many students who would now be accepted somewhere? What educationally significant differences must be taken into account when considering the "fit" between students and institutions or between students and educational programs?

Planning must be based, also, on the requirements of an industrialized, democratic society for specialized personnel and an educated citizenry. Can these needs be met by the generous education of a highly selected, highly able group at the top, or will many kinds and levels of talent and education be needed? Since the task of higher education will be enormous, in number and diversity of students, in educational services, and in research—what division of labor among colleges and universities would be economical and productive? What pattern of institutions, especially public institutions, will best serve our needs? Finally, since planning must be based on judgment concerning the degree of orderliness or rationalization attainable in public systems of higher education without unduly compromising institutions' initiative, autonomy, and distinctiveness—how can the efforts of public colleges and universities in a state be effectively coordinated?

These are the questions discussed in the following pages.

II THE FUTURE SELECTIVITY OF AMERICAN HIGHER EDUCATION

Planning for the future should be based on what seems to be an inescapable assumption, namely, that in the long run American higher education as a whole will not become more selective.

HOW SELECTIVE IS HIGHER EDUCATION NOW?

The Center for the Study of Higher Education attempted to estimate the general selectivity of American higher education by securing the scholastic aptitude test scores of the freshmen of 1952 in a representative national sample of post-high-school institutions and by relating the ability of the entrants to that of high school graduates and the general population. (The sample included 200 institutions.) Later, in order to estimate changes in selectivity, the Center asked the same institutions to supply test scores for the class entering in 1959. In 1952 about 73 per cent of the freshmen came from the upper half of high school graduates in ability; thus a little more than a fourth of the students were drawn from the lower half. In 1959 about 77 per cent of the freshmen from the 167 institutions which supplied data came from the upper half of high school graduates. (The mean score of the freshmen in the 167 colleges in 1952 was the same as that in the entire sample of 200 institutions.) High school graduates, of course, are more capable than the corresponding age group as a whole. The Center estimated that about 95 per cent of college entrants in 1952, and 97 per cent in 1959, were from the upper half of the general population of seventeen-year-olds in ability.[1]

REASONS FOR MOUNTING ENROLLMENT

The percentage of high-ability students who go to college has been increasing, and presumably most young people in the highest quarter of high school graduates will take advantage of some form of higher education in the not too distant future.[2] Many have hoped that these additional capable students would replace the less able ones who are not "college material." This is certainly a vain hope if two-thirds or three-fourths of American youths stream toward the campuses. It is probably also a vain hope if only half of them do, because sharp selection in terms of some basic measure of college aptitude is unlikely to occur in all institutions.

Some of the reasons for expecting a very large and heterogeneous enrollment in higher education have been set forth by the Educational Policies Commission. It pointed out, first, that there will be a large absolute increase in enrollment if only the present percentage of the college-age group continues to enroll; second,

[1] J. G. Darley, *Distribution of Scholastic Ability in Higher Education,* unpublished manuscript, Center for the Study of Higher Education, University of California, Berkeley.

[2] Havighurst reports that in a midwestern city only half of the ablest quarter of youths went to college in 1950 but that two-thirds went in 1960. See R. J. Havighurst, *American Higher Education in the 1960's,* The Ohio State University Press, Columbus, Ohio, 1960, p. 32.

that the pressures to enter and to stay longer are increasing, with the result that a larger percentage of youths will attend and complete college; third, that colleges and universities will respond to social and economic pressures from students, parents, and employers for new programs in general and technical education. These new programs, in turn, will attract greater numbers of students.[3]

The last statement suggests that higher education never quite catches up with potential enrollment. Establishing a new institution in a large population center not only meets an otherwise unsatisfied current demand for higher education but stimulates additional students to seek admission. Frequently, when a new public four-year institution was established in a metropolitan area, the estimates of college attendance had to be raised substantially.

SHORT- VERSUS LONG-RUN TRENDS

It is important to note the qualifications "in the long run" and "as a whole" in the above-stated assumption that higher education will not become more selective. Expansion in the number and size of institutions will probably not keep pace with demand, and *in the short run,* higher education may be able to limit the intake by raising admission standards. (Some institutions will employ the alternative device of restricting output by eliminating a larger percentage of students after admission.) Some private institutions, blessed with a larger pool of applicants, may be able to raise the level of academic ability of their students.[4]

---

[3] *Higher Education in a Decade of Decision,* Educational Policies Commission, Washington, 1957, p. 28.

[4] A few private colleges may be able to improve the academic quality of their student bodies sufficiently to join the elite group of institutions. These are colleges which already draw a substantial share of able students and which, as the crush of students comes, will have enough applicants to raise their standards of admission still higher. They are colleges which

Many public four-year institutions may also be able to raise their admission standards in some degree; some have already done so, and others are likely to follow. The University of Texas, for example, has recently begun selective admission. Pennsylvania State University has decided to admit only the upper 40 per cent of high school graduates. Under a new master plan just adopted in California, the University of California, which is already highly selective, and the state colleges will raise their standards. Recently, about 15 per cent of the graduates of the state's high schools have been eligible for admission to the university, and 45 per cent to the state colleges, at the time of high school graduation. (Other graduates could become eligible after a period in junior colleges or other four-year institutions.) The new plan is to admit as freshmen to the university only the highest twelfth of eligible high school graduates and as freshmen to the state colleges only the upper third.

The University of California could not have become so selective without the system of state colleges, which admit students with a wider range of ability, and junior colleges, which are essentially unselective. In turn, the state colleges could not make even the proposed modest increase in standards of admission if the junior colleges were not widely available (usually in the same communities). The existence of sixty-nine junior colleges makes it possible for the public four-year institutions to reject a student without denying him an opportunity for higher education. This is a cardinal factor in maintaining a selective state college and university system in the face of widespread public demand for access to higher education. The University of Texas would probably have been unable to restrict admission without the existence

---

now place a high premium on intellectual interests and attainments and which already have a substantial number of distinguished faculty members. Obviously, they are institutions that now have a strong financial base and are capable of strengthening it dramatically. Finally, they are institutions which can turn a sound reputation into a widely held image of excellence.

of a varied and fairly extensive system of other public four-year institutions and junior colleges. If major public universities in states where no such network exists raise their entrance standards substantially, it may be predicted that other institutions, such as community colleges, will be established sooner or later to serve a wider range of students.

AN ARGUMENT FOR INCREASING SELECTIVITY

Dr. Robert J. Havighurst has recently taken issue with the widely prevalent belief that a larger percentage of youths will go to college.[5] He considered it is even possible that the percentage will decrease, in spite of the imminent sharp rise in college-age population. His argument may be summarized briefly as follows:

Our economy of high productivity has caused a significant shift in the occupational distribution. The percentage of workers in the upper classes of the occupational hierarchy has increased at the expense of jobs in the lower categories. (Havighurst compressed the census classification into seven occupational groups in his analysis.) Between 1910 and 1950, the percentage of persons in the first category, those engaged in the higher or learned professions, increased slightly. The percentage doubled in the second category, comprising proprietors, officials, and managers in manufacturing, bankers, stockbrokers, engineers, scientists, clergymen, college teachers, and state and Federal officials. There was also a substantial increase in the third category, consisting of school teachers, musicians, trained nurses, retail merchants, salesmen, city and county officials, other proprietors and managers, semi-professional workers, and owners of large farms. There was a slight decrease in the fourth category, comprising clerks, salesmen in offices and stores, stenographers, foremen, locomotive engineers, and owners of medium-sized farms. There was like-

[5] Havighurst, *op. cit.*

wise a small decrease in the fifth category, which included skilled workers, policemen, firemen, mail clerks and carriers, delivery men, cooks, and farmers with mortgages. The sixth category— semiskilled workers, factory operatives, and truck drivers—increased greatly, while the percentage of unskilled laborers, in category seven, decreased.

The great increase in college attendance and graduation since 1930, and especially since World War II, corresponded with large increases in the percentage of the working force in categories two and three. These increases accounted for the great demand in the 1950s for people with college training—a demand which considerably outstripped the supply.

In estimating the future demand for people with college background, Havighurst assumed that the percentage of workers in the highest category would remain stationary. He assumed also that about two-thirds of the positions in the first three categories together would be "appropriate" for college graduates, and he estimated that the percentages of the working force in the second category would increase from 6.5 in 1960 to 7.8 in 1970 and 9 in 1980, and in the third category, from 19 to 21 and 23. He anticipated a slight reduction in categories four to seven and took the position, in any case, that the occupations in these categories would not be "appropriate" for college graduates or men and women with lesser college training.

Havighurst did point out, however, that after World War II the percentage of children from upper-working-class families who attended college increased steadily until 20 per cent had enrolled. In absolute numbers, these young people exceeded the children of upper-class families. Havighurst assumed that lower-class children attended college primarily as a means of qualifying for better jobs and that if the possibility of social and economic mobility through college attendance faded, these children would go to work after finishing high school.

Havighurst contended that vocational opportunities for youths from the lower classes would sharply decline. Three conditions would bring this about. First, the supply of college-trained people would probably meet the demand in 1960 and exceed it thereafter. Second, changes in the fertility of the social classes would discourage college attendance by children from working-class families. Whereas the children of middle-class families were formerly not numerous enough to fill positions for which college education was necessary or desirable and children from the lower classes met the deficiency, increased fertility of the middle class since the war will provide young people to move into middle-class adult positions and thus decrease need for recruits from below. Faced with these barriers to better positions and status, working-class children, except those with exceptionally strong motivation, will not choose to go to college. Third, the small anticipated increase in positions filled by women will not provide an economic incentive for a great increase in college attendance by girls.

Havighurst conceded that certain factors might in part offset the loss of vocational incentives for college attendance as the supply of trained personnel exceeded the demand. Higher education as a means of personal fulfillment and enjoyment—a "consumer good" rather than a "means of production"—might stimulate a study of the liberal arts. Rising levels of education might create new interests and new wants which could be supplied mainly by further education. But these values, Havighurst maintained, would not go far in sustaining college enrollment from the lower classes when its economic advantages had all but disappeared.

The consequence of a prospective oversupply of college-trained workers, Havighurst concluded, will be increased selectivity in college admission to the point of confining college students in the 1960s to those from the upper half of high school graduates in both academic ability and socioeconomic status, unless compensating bases of selection are adopted. While the absolute number enrolled in higher institutions of all types will be much larger, the percentage of the age group in attendance, instead of increasing as is generally assumed, will either remain stable at the present level or decline slightly.

FLAWS IN THE CASE FOR GREATER SELECTIVITY

This assumption is different from the one with which this chapter opened. In the writer's judgment—which may be wrong, since both economic predictions and enrollment projections often turn out to be wide of the mark—there are flaws in Havighurst's argument. First, he has underestimated the demand for college graduates in the upper and lower classes. Why should society be satisfied in the future with the same percentage of workers in the learned professions which now exists? The demand for health services, for example, is related to the people's economic resources. As these resources rise, the desire for medical and dental care, including preventive services, is almost certain to grow. The prediction that only about two-thirds of the jobs in Havighurst's categories two and three will be deemed "appropriate" for college graduates seems much too conservative in the light of steadily mounting educational requirements in positions once thought to require no college training. If college graduation is not required in many of these jobs, some college background will probably be either required or preferred.

The assumption that college training will not be expected or desired in many positions in categories four and five also seems unjustified. It is not hard to envision college-educated factory foremen (or factory operatives, for that matter) as industry substitutes for skilled workers men with the greater knowledge necessary to supervise the intricate machine processes of automation. Many studies have pointed out that a great expansion in the number of technicians will be required. Most jobs on modern farms, even medium-sized ones, call for more scientific know-how and ability to keep abreast of advances in agricultural production than the ownership of farms or the better positions in large-scale agricultural enterprises once demanded. Well-educated stenographers and secretaries, who always seem to be in short supply, will continue to make life easier for executives. Law enforcement should be more effective when policemen are better educated; in the future, many cities may follow the lead of Berkeley, California, which recently set two years of college work as a requirement for appointment to the police force.

There seems little reason to expect a reversal of the trend for employers to ask for some college training in an increasing number of jobs, regardless of the knowledge or special skills required. In many instances, specific training is not necessary; what is wanted is simply greater maturity. If the supply of workers considerably exceeds the demand, educational requirements are usually raised, and prolongation of schooling is the only means of meeting the competition. Elevating educational qualifications (at least in terms of length or amount of formal schooling) is a means, not only of controlling the entrants to an occupation, but also of giving it prestige. One of the major state universities has a two-year curriculum for morticians, and the head of this program once tried to persuade the university's college of liberal arts to approve a four-year combined course. This seems absurd, but it illustrates a widespread social phenomenon in the United States.

Not only do many occupations require more education, but vocational training has been constantly pushed higher in the educational system. Technical and semiprofessional curricula in the junior colleges have displaced trade training in the high school. In California, the junior colleges have complained that the four-year state colleges are invading their vocational domain. And in social work, business administration, and public administration, specialization is being increasingly reserved for the graduate schools.

At still another point Havighurst's predictions seem not to have taken into account possible future changes in college attendance. He assumed that the percentage of women in categories one to three would not change from 1950 to 1980. But if the emphasis continues on preparing women for higher-level positions when their family responsibilities make it possible—rather than for the lesser jobs for which they now so often settle and for which they are now so often trained [6]—then the percentage of women going to college may increase. Furthermore, the many college women who do not enter the labor market represent a group whose motivation in going to college is not mainly vocational; college attendance of such women will depend more on the economic status of their families than on the labor market. As more families are financially able to send their daughters to college, more women may be expected to go for social status or personal improvement.

Finally, Havighurst's argument fails to recognize the social forces—the desire for status and prestige, for social experience, for some of the superficial marks if not the intrinsic values of higher education, as well as for its economic benefits—that have propelled so many young people into the colleges and will continue to do so. We are rapidly approaching the time when going to college will be as customary in American society as going to high school.

WHO WILL DETERMINE HOW MANY WILL GO?

If the social pressures referred to above have been gauged correctly, we may conclude that students and parents will tolerate enrollment restrictions in public higher institutions only for a short time. Eventually they will demand either that existing institutions reopen their doors or that new institutions be established that will admit those barred from selective colleges and

[6] A study of the fields of specialization of women in Minnesota colleges has shown that their apparent vocational aspirations are much lower than their academic ability would justify. Darley, *op. cit.*

universities. Educators might as well face the fundamental fact that it will not be up to them alone to determine how many young people will go to college in the future. In the long run, society will make that decision. In the United States the decision will be to educate the many rather than the few, to send a greater percentage rather than a smaller one to some kind of higher institution. Mass education is here to stay. American higher education will become more rather than less inclusive. This means that the educational system will have to serve an enormously diverse population, a student body certainly no less heterogeneous than the one we have now.

III THE DIVERSE STUDENT BODY
OF AMERICAN HIGHER EDUCATION

Planning for the future must take into account the basic fact that whatever system of higher education emerges from the effort to assimilate 11 million or even 7 million students, will need to be adapted, not only to great variation in academic aptitude and achievement, but also to highly diverse social and cultural backgrounds, interests, and dispositions.

This is a trite axiom, honored more widely in the breach than the observance. Most educators have not even stopped to ask what characteristics significantly affect the educational process, or what characteristics, other than grades, are important outcomes of education.

Until recently, most studies of the diversity of student characteristics in colleges and universities have been concerned with differences in scores on tests of scholastic aptitude or differences in scholastic achievement. This information is obviously important, since differences in academic aptitude and ability are moderately related to differences in subsequent academic attainment. The student's level of scholastic aptitude at any one time, his ultimate altitude, and his rate of growth condition what he can gain from an educational experience. The intellectually abler person, other things being equal, will learn more things, learn more difficult tasks, and learn them more rapidly than the less able one. Robert M. Hutchins once insisted that under effective teaching all students could master the great books. The evidence is clearly to the contrary. Teaching that stretches students' minds in dealing with difficult material may be expected to increase rather than decrease the variability in their attainment.

Of late, interest in higher education has included student characteristics other than academic aptitude and scholastic success. This interest stems from several sources. One is the evidence that measured scholastic aptitude, or even previous scholastic achievement, is in only a limited degree related to college success, expressed either in persistence or in grade-point averages. It is becoming increasingly apparent that the social and cultural background of students, the poverty or the wealth and variety of their previous experience, condition their educational development. Their attitudes, values, intellectual dispositions, and educational goals will likewise help determine how they respond to instruction, to student and faculty culture, to the dominant characteristics of the institutions they attend. A student whose motivation in attending college is primarily vocational may not perform well in a college which stresses general and liberal education and which mainly attracts students interested in ideas rather than practical values.

It would be unfortunate if the college looked upon attitudes, values, and intellectual interests or dispositions as essentially static traits to be coped with in inducing students to meet formal academic requirements. Education, broadly conceived, should *change* attitudes and values toward greater maturity. The goal is a student who, in Dr. Harold Webster's words, is ". . . flexible and realistic in his relations with others; unromantic but at the same time uncynical; kind and impunitive generally, but capable of aggression when it is appropriate; tolerant and undogmatic but not merely in accordance with some uncritical policy or ideology; and personally free, without requiring rules or rituals for managing social relationships."

Webster has observed that data secured by the Center for the Study of Higher Education have shown that this kind of maturity is likely to be associated with serious interest in ideas, in the appreciation and enjoyment of literature and the arts, and in the intellectual life generally.[1]

The origin and development of attitudes and values are still obscure. Jacob, in a widely read survey of published and unpublished research, concluded that except in a limited number of colleges with a distinctive atmosphere, students change little in these fundamental characteristics.[2] Yet, although students' attitudes and values are frequently well defined and firmly established when they reach college, striking changes in individual orientation do occur, and these changes represent the attainment of significant educational objectives.[3]

Attitudes and values, then, are not only factors that condition learning; they are themselves the objects of education. Much of what happens in college may be thought of as the subtle interplay of attitudes, values, interests, and dispositions both as instrumental factors and as outcomes of educational experience.

In the following discussion, diversity, not only in students' ability, but also in their attitudes, values, interests, and intellectual dispositions, will be emphasized. The limiting or facilitating effect

[1] H. Webster, "The Effects of College Education on Personality," unpublished manuscript, Center for the Study of Higher Education, University of California, Berkeley.
[2] P. E. Jacob, *Changing Values in College,* The Edward W. Hazen Foundation, New Haven, Conn., 1956.
[3] N. Sanford (issue editor), "Personality Development during the College Years," *The Journal of Social Issues,* vol. 12, no. 4, 1956. Also H. Webster, "Changes in Attitudes during College," *Journal of Educational Psychology,* vol. 49, pp. 109–117, June, 1958.

of these attributes in development during the college years, and changes in the attributes themselves, will be the subjects of future reports.

Differences among students can be analyzed for the entire population of colleges and universities, as the Center has done in its study of the selectivity of higher education as a whole; or they can be studied by exploring the differential selectivity of groups of institutions; or by exploring variation in single institutions. We shall be primarily concerned with differential selectivity among institutions and, less fully, with examples of diversity in particular institutions. Data on differences both among and within institutions are relevant to basic decisions that should be made about the future pattern of institutions in a diversified system of higher education and about internal educational differentiation. The discussion that follows will deal first with differences in student characteristics from one institution or one group of institutions to another, beginning with the differences best known—those in academic aptitude and ability.

DIFFERENTIAL SELECTIVITY
IN ACADEMIC ABILITY

About a fourth of the freshmen of 1952 in the Center's representative national sample of post-high-school institutions came from the lower half of high school graduates in ability. These less able students contribute to the great variation in measured scholastic aptitude in American higher education. Some notion of the range of talent can be gained from figures A, B, and C in Figure 1, which shows the distribution of ability among the freshmen in three institutions—the least selective and the most selective in the 1952 national sample, and one with an average freshman score approximately equivalent to the average of all students in the sample. The wide part of each bar shows the range within which about two-thirds of the students' scores fell; the thin line extends to the highest and lowest scores in each of the three institutions, and the cross line represents the mean freshman score.

Figures *A, B,* and *C* in Figure 1 show that there was no overlap between institutions A and B in the range of scores marking out about two-thirds of the distributions and relatively little overlap between institutions B and C. The figures in broken lines (Figure 1), *A', B',* and *C',* represent the ranges within which about two-thirds of the freshman scores fell in the same institutions in the autumn of 1959. The mean scores (represented by the horizontal lines through the bars) moved upward between 1952 and 1959 in all three institutions, but in 1959 there was no overlap among the ranges within which about two-thirds of the scores fell.

Figure I
Distributions of ACE Psychological
Test Scores of Freshman in Three
Institutions in 1952 and 1959

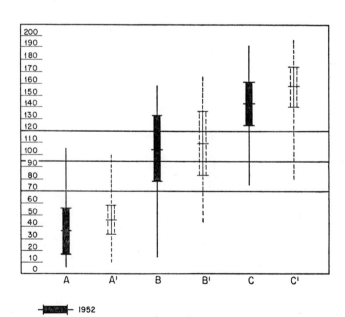

Figure 2 shows the distribution of the *mean* freshman scores in the 200 institutions of the entire 1952 national sample as well as the distribution of individual scores of all students in the sample.

It is well known that the average academic ability of student bodies varies greatly among institutions, but the extent of the variation is often not realized. The Center found that the range of *mean* freshman scholastic aptitude scores among institutions (excluding Negro colleges) in the 1952 national sample was about as great as the range within which three-fourths of the *individual* freshman scores in the entire sample fell. In one state studied by the Center, only 16 per cent of the freshmen in the least selective

Figure II
Distribution of Individual ACE
Psychological Test Scores and
of School Means in a National
Sample of Institutions of Higher Education

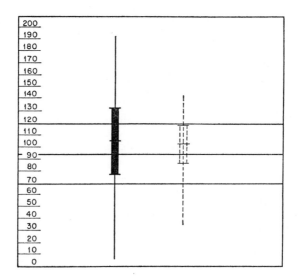

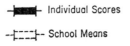
Individual Scores

School Means

institution had scores above the average score in the most selective one. Both institutions are separate liberal arts colleges. Although the two colleges profess comparable objectives, they are most dissimilar in the intellectual demands they can make on their students. The most selective college sends many students on to professional and graduate schools. The other sends few. Yet the curricular pattern of the two institutions is much the same. One might well ask whether the least selective college might not devise an educational program more nearly relevant to the abilities of its students and their future places in society. Such a program, for example, might put more emphasis on general education and less on specialization. It might aim less at the training of experts or the production of scholars than at educating the ordinary student whom it would send out, in the words of Sir Richard Livingstone, "to do the ordinary work of life, with some knowledge of some branch of literature, or learning, a sense of great ideals and achievements, a touch at least of the wisdom, disinterestedness and inspiration which belong to the world of the mind and the spirit."

We have come to expect wide differences in student ability among undergraduate colleges, but the variation at advanced levels is surprising. One might suppose, for example, that there would be little variation in mean scholastic aptitude among medical schools. Medical school students, either freshmen or seniors, are, of course, a select group compared with college freshmen. Yet the mean equivalent score on the American Council on Education Psychological Examination of seniors in the least selective medical school in 1956 was only slightly above the mean of undergraduate college entrants in 1952. Sixteen per cent of the entire group of medical seniors had equivalent ACE scores *below* the mean of college freshmen in general.[4]

[4] The basic data are provided in H. H. Gee, "Differential Characteristics of Student Bodies: Implications for the Study of Medical Education," in T. R. McConnell (ed.), *Selection and Educational Differentiation,* Field Service Center and Center for the Study of Higher Education, University of California, Berkeley, 1960, pp. 125–154.

DIFFERENTIAL SELECTIVITY
IN STUDENTS' VALUES

Only a limited number of examples of diversity in students' values can be given here. Again, this subject will be approached through evidence on differential selectivity or attraction among various institutions and groups of institutions.

In a study conducted at Cornell University, students in several colleges and universities were asked to choose from a list of possible educational goals those they thought the ideal institution should emphasize. The responses varied from institution to institution. For example, students at Wesleyan, Yale, Harvard, and Dartmouth were most likely to check "basic general education and appreciation of ideas" and least likely to stress vocational training. On the other hand, men at the state universities included in the study checked vocational education much more frequently than those at the Ivy League colleges.[5]

It is interesting to speculate on possible reasons for the apparent differential drawing power of the two groups of institutions. Perhaps students who attend Ivy League colleges simply can *afford* to have or to profess an interest in liberal studies or to take time to go through the motions. Their parents may have the financial resources to give them a liberal education before the students turn to specialization or vocational preparation. Perhaps, too, many of them look forward to positions in their fathers' firms for which professional education is not necessary. On the other hand, students in state universities may more frequently be forced by financial necessity to turn immediately to vocational objectives. But it is also possible that the professed interest of many Ivy League students in "general education and appreciation of ideas" is real, and that therefore they are likely

[5] Rose K. Goldsen, Morris Rosenberg, Robin M. Williams, Jr., and Edward A. Suchman, *What College Students Think*, D. Van Nostrand Company, Inc., Princeton, N.J., 1960, p. 208.

to choose institutions which are noted for liberal studies rather
than vocational education. The general public image of state
universities is, in contrast, that vocational education is their primary business.

The Center has comparable data for 900 exceptionally able
men and women who received National Merit Scholarship Corporation awards in 1956. About 50 per cent of those who entered
public institutions said they were primarily interested in vocational training, whereas only 25 per cent of those who went to
private and Protestant institutions and 17 per cent of those who
attended Roman Catholic institutions were so oriented. By contrast, only 38 per cent of the NMSC students who chose public
institutions said they were interested primarily in intellectual
matters; but 60, 53, and 40 per cent, respectively, of those who
attended the other three groups of institutions expressed this
dominant interest. It is reasonable to assume that the NMSC
students who said their primary purpose was to secure a "basic
general education and appreciation of ideas" were sincerely interested in intellectual affairs and liberal studies.

These studies in students' values have been corroborated, at
least indirectly, by the Center's studies of the differences in intellectual disposition of NMSC students who attended different
groups of institutions. On a test of "thinking introversion"
designed to measure liking for reflective thought and interest in
ideas as ideas rather than in their practical applications, NMSC
students who attended public universities had lower scores than
those who went to liberal arts colleges, Ivy League universities,
and other private universities. The NMSC students as a group
made higher scores on this test than college students in general,
and the differences from one group of institutions to another,
though "statistically significant" (that is, unlikely to have occurred by chance), were absolutely small.

Further indirect corroborative evidence on differential selectivity in educational values and attitudes was found by the

Center. A doctoral student, working there with data on the NMSC students, devised a method of scoring responses on the Strong Vocational Interest Blank [6] for theoretical and applied orientations. These characteristics he conceived to be bipolar dimensions of intellectual disposition.

By theoretical disposition he meant "a preference for the abstract and speculative, and the satisfaction to be gained from the interplay of ideas. Individuals in whom such preferences are strong might be expected to gain satisfactions from intellectual activities intrinsic to problem-solving tasks, or to enjoy learning for its own sake."

By applied disposition he meant "a preference for the utilitarian and practical or the satisfactions to be gained from the realization of goals which for some may be more personally 'significant' than pure speculative activity."

This investigator distinguished three groups of NMSC students along a continuum from a highly theoretical to a highly applied orientation. The theoretically inclined group tended to be thoughtful, reflective, independent, creative; responsive to complexities of the environment and to internal impulses; sensitive to others, permissive in relationships, and tolerant in attitudes, although somewhat lacking in determination and persistence. Students in this group chose majors in the natural sciences, humanities, and social sciences about twice as frequently as in the professions or business.

The group with applied inclinations tended to prefer physical activity to reflection. It preferred to deal with the simple and concrete rather than with the complex or intangible; to be identified with power and authority and to be more directive than permissive in its relations with people. Students in this group chose majors almost exclusively in the technical fields and elected engi-

[6] This is an instrument by which a person's professed interests may be compared with the interests of persons who have been successful in various occupations.

neering three times as often as the natural sciences.[7] Students with applied inclinations and immediate vocational goals are much more likely to be found in institutions which offer a wide range of vocational curricula.

Reporting that students in state universities are more interested in vocational curricula than those in other types of institutions is not meant to suggest that the former institutions should give them vocational training and little else. It is meant to imply, rather, that faculties who want to interest students in ideas will have a different problem in the two groups of institutions.

INSTITUTIONAL DIFFERENCES IN STUDENTS'
SOCIAL BACKGROUND

Studies recently conducted under the auspices of the Center have shown that certain groups of educational institutions in Minnesota are differentially selective or attractive not only with respect to academic ability but also with respect to socioeconomic background, as reflected in father's occupation. The state colleges and the junior colleges are attended predominantly by students whose fathers are in "low-status occupations" (which include clerical and lower occupational titles). Thus, only 27 per cent of the men and 21 per cent of the women in the state colleges had fathers in "high-status occupations" (managerial and above). In the private, non-Catholic, coeducational liberal arts colleges, on the other hand, 54 per cent of the men and 56 per cent of the women had fathers in the high-status category.

The father's occupational status plays an important role in determining who goes to college, but it is not significantly related to the persistence of those who enter. Wolfle reported that with the exception of the sons and daughters of farmers, "when college

[7] M. P. Weissman, "An Approach to the Assessment of Intellectual Disposition among Selected High Ability Students," unpublished doctoral dissertation, University of California, Berkeley, 1958.

entrants are classified by the occupations of their fathers the percentages getting degrees are fairly constant." [8] This remains true even when academic ability is taken into account. Darley, in his study of college attendance in Minnesota, investigated the relationship of the father's occupation to persistence in two ability groups, one of which was composed of students at or above the average on high school rank and on scholastic aptitude test scores in the type of institution attended, and the other was below the average on both counts. His general conclusion was that while the father's occupation was clearly related to the type of institution attended, as noted above, it was not significantly related to the percentage earning degrees when academic ability was taken into account. The only differences discovered—and these approached statistical significance—were in the state colleges.[9] Thus there are many good educational risks in the lower social groups.

It seems clear that our manpower needs are such that we cannot justify an educational system built on a two-way break between lower and upper socioeconomic levels if, as Darley's data suggest, the good student in a less intellectually stimulating institution fails to attain his own optimal development or if the poor student in a relatively selective institution fails in tasks beyond the level of his ability.

Utilization of manpower and optimum realization of individual potentialities would seem to require that attendance at a particular institution or type of institution should not depend on the accidents of economic resources or the geographical availability of a certain college. By counseling and by financial assistance, students should be enabled to attend the institution in which they can make the most of their academic ability.

In the meantime, there are other problems than those of capitalizing academic ability in institutions where students come over-

[8] Dael Wolfle, *America's Resources of Specialized Talent*, Harper & Brothers, New York, 1954, p. 160.

[9] J. G. Darley, *Distribution of Scholastic Ability in Higher Education*, unpublished manuscript, Center for the Study of Higher Education.

whelmingly from less privileged homes. The variation in attitudes, beliefs, values, motivation, familiarity with ideas, and
knowledge of the greater society creates, in turn, profound differences in the climates of educational institutions. The enormously complicated task which lack of cultural sophistication
poses to a faculty convinced that students, whatever their origins,
should be initiated into the world of ideas was suggested by Dr.
Martin Trow, a member of the Center's staff, when he said: [10]

> I would suggest that the readiness to deal with ideas as
> things in themselves, and the general knowledge about man
> and his works that is usually associated with that tendency,
> is, so to speak, a necessary if not sufficient condition for a
> liberal education. And moreover, that colleges face very dif-
> ferent problems in the education of youngsters who already
> possess some measure of these attitudes and information be-
> fore they come to college, as compared with those who do
> not. And this, I need not say, is quite independent of general
> intelligence.

Encouraging cultural sophistication should not be equated
with inculcating uncritically *all* middle- or upper-middle-class
values and attitudes. Jacob declared that "the main overall
effect of higher education upon student values is to bring about
general acceptance of a body of standards and attitudes characteristic of college-bred men and women in the American community." He stated, too, that the uniformity of values at the end
is greater than at the beginning of college. "Fewer seniors espouse
beliefs which deviate from the going standards than do freshmen," he concluded, "as a result of which the graduate can fit
comfortably into the ranks of American college alumni." [11]

This kind of uncritical absorption of values and attitudes, this
increasing conformity to the social norm, may only perpetuate

[10] M. Trow, "Cultural Sophistication and Higher Education," in
McConnell (ed.), *op. cit.*, pp. 107–123.
[11] Jacob, *op. cit.*, p. 6.

middle-class smugness instead of leading to the kind of deeper cultural sophistication which Trow had in mind. This sophistication is engendered not only by formal study but also by a college environment rich in intellectual and cultural activities. Institutions which have student bodies with meager backgrounds should make a special effort to bring to their campuses distinguished writers, artists, scholars, and statesmen.

INSTITUTIONAL DIFFERENCES IN STUDENTS' INTELLECTUAL DISPOSITIONS

Evidence has been presented recently that institutions or groups of institutions are differentially selective with respect to intellectual bents or dispositions. For example, colleges with a large percentage of graduates who had become scientists and scholars attracted a group of National Merit Scholarship Corporation winners and runners-up who had higher scores on measures of complexity of outlook and aesthetic values, and lower scores on authoritarian attitudes and religious values, than the NMSC students who attended the less productive colleges. Among the students who had scores well above the mean on measures of both theoretical and aesthetic values, more than twice as many were found in the high-productivity schools as in the low ones.[12]

This combination of theoretical and aesthetic orientation is associated with a creative disposition. For example, the combination appears dramatically in the creative people who have been studied at the Institute for Personality Assessment and Research in the University of California at Berkeley. Some results of these studies have been summarized as follows: [13]

The profiles on the Allport-Vernon-Lindzey *Study of Values* of our creative architects, research scientists, and

[12] T. R. McConnell and P. Heist, "Do Students Make the College?" *College and University*, vol. 34, pp. 442–452, Summer, 1959.
[13] D. W. MacKinnon, "Identifying and Developing Creativity," in McConnell, (ed.), *op. cit.*, pp. 75–89.

mathematicians show a high elevation on both theoretical and aesthetic values. . . . The highest value for research scientists is theoretical (57.0) [14] followed by aesthetic (47.5); for architects the aesthetic value is the highest (56.4) with the theoretical value in second place (50.8); while for the creative mathematicians the two values, still well above average, are approximately equally high (aesthetic 52.9, theoretical 52.0).

Investigations at the Center showed that some colleges draw more students with theoretical interests, and others attract more of those with applied bents. The Center has data on a number of California institutions, two of which lie near the extremes of the colleges in the state on the measures in question. The difference in mean scores between the highest and the lowest colleges on a test of interest in ideas as ideas rather than in their practical consequences was nearly 2 standard deviations; that is to say, the difference in means was about as great as the range which comprised about two-thirds of the *individual* scores in all the institutions. On a test of complexity of outlook, the difference in means was more than 1.3 standard deviations, and on authoritarianism almost 1.5 standard deviations in the reverse direction.

Some institutions, then, have large numbers of students who are intellectually flexible, tolerant of ambiguity, and intrinsically interested in learning; other institutions enroll many with little interest in abstract thinking, with little originality, and with tendencies toward conventional and rigid thought processes.

Saying that education should be adapted to such differences does not mean that an institution should confirm and strengthen the undesirable or limiting characteristics students bring with them; it means, as studies have demonstrated,[15] that a special

[14] The mean for college students in general on the theoretical as well as the other parts of the instrument is approximately 40. Gordon W. Allport, Philip E. Vernon, and Gardner Lindzey, *Study of Values: Manual of Directions*, Houghton Mifflin Company, Boston, 1960, p. 8.

[15] See, for example, G. G. Stern and A. H. Cope, "Differences in

kind of education is needed to lead the rigid, intellectually conventional or dependent student toward more flexible and independent attitudes.

Differences among medical schools in students' scholastic ability were mentioned earlier. Even more interesting are differences among medical schools in the personality characteristics of their students. An example may be taken from an earlier report: [16]

> An inspection of the mean profiles of medical seniors on a single instrument, the Allport-Vernon-Lindzey Study of Values, indicates that it is possible to identify certain characteristic clusters of institutions. For example, three medical colleges, two of which, at least, are noted for the proportion of graduates going into research and teaching, have comparable mean senior profiles: i.e., the students in these schools tend to be similar in orientation and distinctly different from those in other clusters of medical schools. The seniors in these three schools have in common relatively high *theoretical* scores *and* relatively high *aesthetic* scores, both values considerably above the mean of college students in general, and aesthetic scores considerably higher than those in other medical schools. Another group of colleges have in common relatively high theoretical scores but aesthetic scores that approximate the mean of college students in general. Still a third cluster can be distinguished that are still high in theoretical scores but in aesthetic scores are well below the mean of college students in general. A third distinguishing characteristic of these clusters is the mean score on religious values. In the first group of three schools with high theoretical and high aesthetic scores, the religious scores are low; in the last cluster, which had low aesthetic scores, the mean re-

Educability between Stereopaths, non-Stereopaths, and Rationals," *American Psychologist*, vol. 11, p. 362, 1956.
[16] McConnell and Heist, *op. cit.*

ligious score is almost a standard deviation above the mean of college students in general.

Many medical schools, of course, enroll a few students as capable as those in schools which attract exceptionally able students and some students with personality characteristics similar to those which are typical of schools with distinctive student bodies. Should not an attempt be made to attain a better pairing of students and schools, not only in general scholastic aptitude, but also in such factors as theoretical orientation, complexity and originality of thought, creative potential? If this is not done, it is essential for each school to identify the characteristics of individual students and to differentiate their education in a way that will maximize their peculiar potentialities.

Questions raised by the data summarized above have been put as follows:

> Should each medical school try to produce all types of doctors, or should each school try to fulfill a specific mission? For example, should some schools seek to produce practitioners and others researchers and teachers? Should free transfer of students between schools be allowed when a student is not in the school best suited for his educational needs and objectives? . . . Should a man who at the end of his sophomore year is primarily interested in a research career in neuro-physiology remain in a school whose prime goal is the production of general or even specialized practitioners? Or, conversely, should a man primarily interested in general practice continue in a school highly oriented toward academic medicine? [17]

What of the student whose values and personality needs

[17] Cooperative studies at the Center for the Study of Higher Education and the research division of the Association of American Medical Colleges have shown not only that students in some medical colleges

are not consonant with the great majority of those in the school? Should the free transfer of students between schools be allowed, or should the school reevaluate itself in relation to the individual students and try to give each man the type of education he seeks? [18]

INFLUENCE OF THE "STUDENT MIX" [19]
ON INDIVIDUAL ACHIEVEMENT

Little attention has been given to the distribution of students among the institutions of a complex system or among educational programs within a complex institution. This is not to say that distribution of students among educational opportunities is left to chance. Students tend to find their own intellectual level, to seek an education among their intellectual peers, in the diverse maze of colleges and universities. Yet the pairing of students with institutions, in what is and must remain a highly voluntary system of college choice and selection, leaves much to be desired. Many institutions, even some of the more selective ones, are surprisingly heterogeneous in student ability. The Center has found that the variability in general scholastic aptitude in the most and least selective institutions in a midwestern state is about the same. Institutions with student bodies of meager average ability may have a few students of outstanding capacity.

Would these exceptional students more nearly reach their possible level of intellectual development in an institution with

---

have characteristic patterns of personality traits but also that there are differences in the characteristics of students who wish to specialize in certain medical fields, including teaching and research. See Gee, *op. cit.*, pp. 125–154.

[18] D. H. Funkenstein, "The Implications of Diversity," in H. H. Gee and R. J. Glaser (eds.), *The Ecology of the Medical Student,* Association of American Medical Colleges, Evanston, Ill., 1958, pp. 34–58.

[19] This is a term coined by David Riesman.

stiffer academic competition? The early study by Learned and Wood of the academic achievement of students in Pennsylvania colleges suggests that the answer is yes. They reported the gains of a group of superior students from freshman to senior year on a test of general knowledge in the arts and sciences in a college in which the median senior score on the examination was well under the state-wide median. The students chosen for particular study were the fifty freshmen who at the end of their first year had scores superior to those of 72 per cent of the seniors on the eve of graduation from the same college. Of the original number, thirty-four were still in college as juniors. Let Learned and Wood tell the story of the test scores of the latter on reexamination: [20]

> Of the 34 who were tested a second time by the same measure, 23 had lower scores than they had achieved two years previously. The reason for this phenomenon in each individual case is unknown, but the fact that minds of this caliber had been obliged through two years to adjust their stride and intellectual sympathies to colleagues, and probably even to some instructors who were inferior [to] themselves cannot have been without its sinister effect. These students obviously had had no intellectual purpose or stimulus appropriate to their ability. Although as freshmen they were already beyond that intellectual level at which the college could serve them effectively, they were obliged to use their wits elsewhere and mark time academically for three more years until the calendar should release them.

The same investigators studied the performance in two groups of colleges of students who had done equally well on tests taken as high school seniors. Thirty-two liberal arts colleges were divided into two numerically equal groups, A and B, on the basis of total

[20] W. S. Learned and B. D. Wood, *The Student and His Knowledge,* Carnegie Foundation for the Advancement of Teaching, New York, 1938, p. 26.

average scores of their seniors on the college-level tests. Group A was composed of colleges with high average scores; group B of colleges with low averages. The seniors were divided into tenths on the basis of their high school scores, and their performance on the college tests was compared, tenth by tenth, in the two groups of institutions. The students in the highest tenth on the high school tests made average scores of 831 and 785 in the A and B colleges, respectively. Those in the second highest tenth made average scores of 700 and 615. Not only did the ablest students, as determined by their high school tests, do better in the A colleges, but all ten ability groups made higher average scores in these institutions. The average score of students in all tenths in the A colleges was 717 and in the B colleges, 581. The report interprets these results, with appropriate reservations that will not be repeated here, as follows: [21]

> In the B group ... the center of intellectual gravity is low; the median pupil comes from the fourth tenth of high school graduates. Students from the upper strata of ability are few, and have correspondingly less influence on the tone of the institution; they receive less stimulation from their colleagues and teachers, and since with their ability it is easy for them to maintain their honors, they tend to do less work. In the A group, on the other hand, the median student is from the second tenth, the first two tenths contributing about 56 per cent of the total as compared with only 33 per cent drawn from the upper two tenths in the B group. The leaders and pace-setters from these two top tenths, therefore, dominate the institutions; being relatively numerous, they find rivalry and stimulus among their peers, they are compelled to fight for honors, and by their good example they pass the energy with which they are charged down the line.

[21] *Ibid.*, p. 216.

More evidence needs to be adduced before this generalization is firmly established,[22] but until then we may take the conclusion as a likely hypothesis. It would seem to give some support, concerning able students at least, to Henry Wriston's contention that "the ideal college should serve a student body drawn from the narrowest possible range in the scale of ability"; but whether it would be good for the student of lesser but still better-than-average ability to be deprived of the stimulus of exceptional associates is another question. Perhaps it would be better to say that the moral of the Learned and Wood data is not to segregate students narrowly by ability, but to make certain that each mix contains enough able students to stimulate one another and those of lesser ability.

Even in institutions which are highly selective in general academic aptitude, the student bodies may differ significantly in other characteristics related to intellectual disposition and intellectual functioning. This is true, for example, in two distinguished liberal arts colleges. The mean scholastic aptitude test scores of the 1958 freshmen in the two colleges were approximately the same. Yet on measures of complexity, originality, and theoretical and aesthetic values, the mean scores in one of the colleges were significantly higher than in the other. Such institutional differences greatly complicate the problem of determining what setting would be best for a particular student.

THE PROBLEM OF "PAIRING" STUDENTS
AND INSTITUTIONS

Nevertheless, the possibility of attaining a better pairing of students and institutions is receiving increased attention. Obvi-

[22] The Center for the Study of Higher Education is now engaged in a study of student development in eight institutions. In this investigation it will be possible to study the academic histories of high-ability students in institutions which differ markedly in the general level of ability of their student bodies.

ously, no simple system for this will work; there are too many variables to take into account. Among them are the differences among students on any one dimension; the distribution among traits in the individual; and the atmospheres and climates, the structures and functions of the institutions themselves. All we can hope for, probably, is a little more orderly distribution of students among institutions and among educational programs. This is one of the problems discussed in the following chapters.

INTERNAL DIVERSITY

The emphasis in this chapter thus far has been on differences among institutions in the nature of their student bodies; the illustrations should have given some notion of the enormity of the variation in student ability, social and emotional maturity, intellectual disposition, interests, motivations, and values with which American higher education as a whole must cope. But particular institutions also have to contend with various degrees of diversity in all these attributes among their own students. This leads to problems of internal educational differentiation.

A few colleges are fairly homogeneous in student ability, but most institutions admit students who vary widely in academic aptitude and achievement, even though the average may be high. Amherst and the California Institute of Technology admit students within a fairly narrow range of ability. Amherst's report on the admission of freshmen in 1960 showed that 87 per cent of the entrants were from the highest quarter of their high school classes, and another 7 per cent were from the second quarter. About 97 per cent of the admitted freshmen had scores of 500 or higher on the mathematical section of the College Board Scholastic Aptitude Test, which means that practically all were above the mean of the norm group for this examination (and the norm group was undoubtedly above the mean of college freshmen in general). Furthermore, more than 80 per cent had scores higher than 600, the point above which only 16 per cent of the norm group would be expected to fall. At the California Institute of Technology, the freshmen of 1957 had mean Scholastic Aptitude Test scores of 649 and 734 on the verbal and mathematical sections. Only a few of the group had scores in the 500 to 600 range.

Institutions like these are the exceptions. Most colleges and universities are much more heterogeneous. For example, the standard deviations of academic aptitude test scores in the most selective and least selective colleges in a midwestern state were about the same.[23] In the national sample drawn by the Center, the standard deviation of scores in the least selective institution, a southern Negro college, was approximately equal to that in the most selective institution, a private Ivy League university. Although the distributions of scores in the two institutions were probably mutually exclusive and although there was little in common intellectually between them, the problem of adjusting to the range of abilities in entering students was presumably as pressing in the one as in the other. Although freshmen at the University of California are drawn from the top 15 per cent of high school graduates, they vary much more than this would suggest on a test of scholastic aptitude,[24] and they are also diverse in intellectual interests and dispositions. The Berkeley freshmen of 1956 and 1957 had a much higher mean score on the College Classification Test than did freshmen in a large sample of colleges and universities across the nation, but the dispersion of Berkeley scores, while less than that for all institutions combined in the norm group, was still great. About two-thirds of the scores in the normative distribution fell within a range of 62 points around a mean of 121. The same proportion of scores of Berkeley fresh-

---

[23] Within the range of 1 standard deviation on either side of the mean of a normal distribution, about 68 per cent of the cases would be found.

[24] "Test Scores of Berkeley, 'National' Freshmen," *University Bulletin*, vol. 6, no. 27, p. 117, University of California, 1958.

men in the College of Letters and Science was within a range of
46 points around a mean of 145. Although the Berkeley freshmen
were more homogeneous in ability than the norm group, the
spread was still great enough to create problems of educational
differentiation and adaptation. Clearly, students in the selective
University of California should not be treated alike. In less selective state colleges or universities the range of talent is likely to be
even greater. American higher education cannot escape the problem of individualization; although the problem cannot be solved,
it can be made more manageable in some institutions than in
others.

As stated, institutions or groups of institutions are differentially selective with respect to social background. Significant differences also exist within particular institutions, even within the
intellectually more selective ones. The Center is investigating student characteristics and student development at various colleges,
three of which have unusually able student bodies. Yet Trow reported that in these three "elite" colleges about a quarter of the
students own fewer than fifteen books, while another quarter own
more than seventy-five. He went on:

> The range of variation in the number of books in their
> parents' homes is equally wide: in a quarter of their homes
> there are fewer than 100 books of all kinds, while one stu-
> dent in five comes from a home having 600 books or more.
> Moreover, the variation in their knowledge, tastes, and inter-
> ests is extraordinarily wide—extraordinary, that is, in the
> light of the apparent and, I think, superficial similarity in
> their backgrounds. Some know almost nothing about pub-
> lic affairs, while others know a great deal; some report they
> read widely, others confess they get little chance for any
> serious reading; somewhat surprisingly, for students at these
> colleges, almost a quarter report that they have never read
> a book of poetry in their lives; the proportion is about a third

of the boys. And we find the same kinds of variation in their magazine reading, in their preferences in music, and in their sentiments on a wide range of social and political issues.

Trow pointed out that these characteristics are related in the same way they are in the general population. With the ownership of books goes more serious reading, more familiarity with the world at large, less interest in the mass culture, such as popular music and magazines. The freshmen whose cultural interests are like those of college graduates also have comparable attitudes toward social and political issues. They are more tolerant of political and social diversity and are opposed to encroachments on academic freedom.[25]

In discussing diversity among institutions, we have commented on the fact that two colleges—two of the three just referred to—whose student bodies had equally high average scholastic aptitude scores differed significantly in such intellectual characteristics as theoretical and aesthetic orientation, interest in ideas for their own sake, and complexity of outlook. In many ways, however, the diversity within either of the two colleges was more striking than the differences between them. Let us look for a moment at the diversity in the institution with the lower mean freshmen scores on the measures of intellectual disposition in question. Three groups—subcultures, so to speak—have been identified in this college. Let them be designated as groups A, B, and C.[26]

Group A includes the socially oriented, who have a high degree of school spirit, and who tend to emphasize vocational goals; group B are the independents, who are unaffiliated with particular social groups—they seem to be "noncollegiate," but are interested both in their professional subject

[25] Trow, *op. cit.*
[26] P. Heist and H. Webster, "Differential Characteristics of Undergraduate Student Bodies: Implications for Selection and the Study of Undergraduates," in McConnell, *op. cit.*, pp. 91–106.

fields and in the social and political issues of the day; and group C are the intellectual liberals, who tend to be critical nonconformists, many of them chiefly interested in the humanities and in the creative arts.

The mean standard scores of the three groups on two scales were as follows:

Scales	Sophomore averages		
	Group A	Group B	Group C
Interest in ideas	57.8	59.3	67.3
Complexity of outlook	57.0	62.6	67.3

The mean scores of group C on measures both of interest in ideas and of complexity of outlook are well above the mean scores for the entire freshman class. One wonders whether the members of group C would reach their potentialities better in a college where they were associated with students with considerably lower scores on the measures in question or in an environment of peers with attitudes more like their own. Little is known about the right "student mix" for a given institution. It is obvious, however, that the college should identify students like those in group C and, by whatever special treatment may be productive, stimulate them to realize their intellectual and creative potential.

Until more is known about objective methods for selecting students on grounds other than academic aptitude and previous scholastic success, most institutions which choose freshmen on the basis of theoretical disposition or creative potential will be privately controlled. For the time being, the problem of most public universities, whatever the general intellectual level of their student bodies, will be to identify students with special aptitudes and varied dispositions, styles, or potentialities and to differentiate their educational experience in accordance with their individual qualities or advise them to transfer to other institutions.

It will be pointed out later that in a differentiated system of public higher education there may be graduated standards of academic aptitude for admission from one type of institution to another, with least selectivity in community colleges and the greatest in the state university. But each institution in the system, whatever the *general* level of ability of its student body, will still have to cope with a fairly wide range of talent. Furthermore, if a single institution offers varied curricula, it will have the problem of aiding students to choose among these programs in accordance not only with their general scholastic aptitude and previous achievement but also with their particular interests, special aptitudes, and basic characteristics of personality. A differentiated educational system thus must conjure with individual differences both among and within the institutions of which it is composed.

IV AMERICAN SOCIETY REQUIRES TRAINING IN DEPTH

Another proposition on which future arrangements for higher education should be based is that a democratic, industrialized society needs many types and levels of talent and education.

Some critics regard the provision of education beyond the high school for a large segment of American youth as an absurdity if not a catastrophe. A distinguished literary scholar has compared the influx of college students to the barbarian invasions of the Middle Ages and has declared that mass education leads inevitably to education for none.[1] If education for the many does spawn mediocrity, the results may indeed be catastrophic. Unless education challenges the brilliant while serving the ordinary, it will ultimately condemn us to a mean estate.

Yet a democratic, industrialized society cannot exist and grow through the efforts of an elite alone, even though the few be selected on the basis of intelligence rather than privilege. This society rests on the service of citizens whose talents are few or

[1] Douglas Bush, "Education for All Is Education for None," *New York Times Magazine*, Jan. 9, 1955, pp. 13–14.

modest together with those whose abilities are many or exceptional.

Speaking recently of the importance in American society of many echelons of ability, training, and skill, Dr. John Gardner, president of the Carnegie Corporation, pointed out that the nation needs not only creative scientists who win Nobel prizes but also able scientists and mathematicians at many lower levels. Behind the great creative minds are required an enormous number of highly able and excellently educated scientists to conduct a wide range of researches, as well as the lesser men who do the unspectacular work but who accumulate the vast array of data which support the structure of science. All these efforts are supplemented by a great corps of technicians and assistants.

Dr. Gardner observed that the industrial world is comparably organized. At the top and in the headlines are "the great designers, inventors, and innovators" who set the stage for the able technologists who translate their discoveries into practical operations. Behind these men are technicians and mechanics—the hands of the higher echelons. Only recently, said Gardner, have we learned that the strength of American industry and of the nation's economy lies in this "training in depth." Other nations may match us in the production of brilliant scientists and engineers, but America surpasses them in the training of competent second-, third-, fourth-, and fifth-level workers.[2]

SHORTAGE OF TECHNICIANS AND ENGINEERS IN ENGLAND

In England the number of young people who attain both advanced and intermediate levels of education, or even education as technicians, is still relatively small. At the beginning of the academic year 1958–1959 only 14,942 students of technology at-

[2] J. Gardner, "Commentary: Mathematics in Crisis," *Quarterly Report*, Carnegie Corporation of New York, January, 1956.

tended the universities of Britain. Beneath—for the most part until very recently, far beneath—the universities, local technical colleges are widely available in the industrial communities of the country. But the work in many of them has been predominantly elementary—many of them have accepted students at the end of the compulsory school age of fifteen—and has been conducted mainly on a part-time basis. In 1957–1958 the technical colleges enrolled only 90,256 full-time students. The remainder were either evening students (997,552) or part-time day students (485,319) on limited released time from industry.[3]

It is possible for British students to complete the academic requirements for technical or professional qualifications by the part-time route, but the number of those who finish the course is small, although each year about one in six of the scientists and two out of three of the new crop of engineers meet their academic requirements in a technical college. It has been estimated that—at best—of those who start the program, only one in five earns an Ordinary National Certificate (which is now somewhat below, but is to be raised to, the level of a technician's certificate) ; and but one in seven completes the requirements for the Higher National Certificate, which is prerequisite to the attainment of full professional qualification as a scientist or technologist, such as membership in the Institution of Electrical Engineers. One can only conclude, with an expert on technical education, that "the system of technical education is far too dependent on part-time education to meet modern and future needs."[4] The number produced is far too small, and the process takes much too long.

It became increasingly apparent that the failure of the universities and technical colleges together to produce a sufficient num-

---

[3] The usual pattern is one day a week on the employer's time and one evening on the employee's time.

[4] P. F. R. Venables, "Technical Education," *Journal of the Royal Society of Arts,* vol. 108, pp. 30–47, December, 1959. The statistics on enrollment are taken from this source.

ber of applied scientists and engineers had seriously handicapped technological progress and economic development in Great Britain. Following a series of reports on scientific manpower by various working parties, the Ministry of Education presented the White Paper on Technical Education to Parliament in 1956. This report recognized that the universities should expand their technological departments but agreed that they should not and could not do so sufficiently to meet the need.

The White Paper therefore urged that technological education outside the universities be greatly expanded. More particularly, it proposed that certain technical colleges—those which were already carrying a fairly extensive load of advanced instruction and which had, or could recruit, well-qualified faculties—be transformed into colleges of advanced technology.

The program began by the creation of eight such colleges, which were required gradually to transfer their elementary work to other technical colleges then in existence or to be created. Presumably, the colleges of advanced technology were to provide instruction in applied science and engineering at the university level, but in different ways, particularly in close association with the principal industries in their areas.[5] Degrees are the monopoly of the universities in Britain; therefore, the credential for graduates of the colleges is called Diploma in Technology.

In addition to the creation of colleges of advanced technology,

[5] The more optimistic proponents of the advanced colleges of technology stated that these institutions will produce graduates comparable in quality to those who meet the standards for second-class honors in the universities. This writer's observation was that in most colleges this was a goal that would be attained, if at all, only over a considerable period of time. The fact that these new colleges are not permitted to confer degrees, which are still to be restricted to the universities, gives them an immediate handicap which is not likely to be easily overcome. The National Council on Technological Awards was established for the recognition of courses and the making of awards. This council decided to grant the Diploma in Technology to students who met its requirements.

some departments in other technical colleges which had strong staffs and which gave a considerable amount of advanced work, were approved for courses leading to the diploma in technology, and other departments will reach such status in the future. Additional colleges of advanced technology may be designated as need dictates and quality permits. The ninth, as a matter of fact, has been named. A system of part-time education, though of a sort very different from the day-release plan, is, however, to be continued. The programs of the advanced colleges of technology are, for the most part, organized as "sandwich courses," in which the student alternates between six months in full-time study at the college and six months in the factory or firm. Most of the students are "works-based"; that is, the student first gets a job and, if properly qualified, may be permitted to take a sandwich course at the college. Others are college-based (the number of these is small, but is to be increased), and still others, although a relatively small number, are full-time college students. In most instances, the employer pays the student in a sandwich course his regular wage while he is in school, which makes engineering training feasible for many who would otherwise find it financially impossible to secure a professional education.

The creation of the colleges of advanced technology may be expected to reduce appreciably Britain's deficit in engineering manpower. The Ministry of Education has also taken steps to strengthen the entire system of technical education by establishing a hierarchy of institutions leading progressively from local to area to regional colleges, with the colleges of advanced technology as the apex of the system. But lack of technologists below the top layer, or the top two layers, of engineers and the great deficit in personnel at the level of technician—the level supplied in part in the United States by junior colleges and two-year technical institutes—will still remain a severe handicap in industrial development.

The distinguished British scientist and novelist C. P. Snow, after commenting recently on the fact that a very small percentage of his country's youths enter the universities, pointed out that in his judgment the Russians have better insight into the types and levels of training an industrialized society requires. This is his analysis: [6]

> The Russians have judged what kind and number of educated men and women a country needs to come out on top in the scientific revolution. . . . First of all, as many alpha-plus scientists as the country can produce. No country has many of them. . . .
>
> Second, a much larger stratum of alpha professionals— these are the people who are going to do the supporting research, the high class design and development. . . . Third, another stratum, educated to about the level of Part I of the Natural Sciences or Mechanical Sciences Tripos, or perhaps slightly below that. Some of these will do the secondary technical jobs, but some will take major responsibility, particularly in the human jobs. . . . As the scientific revolution goes on, the call for these men will be something we haven't imagined, though the Russians have. They will be required in thousands upon thousands, and they will need all the human development that university education can give them.

A MORE RATIONALLY DIFFERENTIATED SYSTEM
NEEDED IN THE UNITED STATES

The need for technological training in depth might suggest that in the United States we should have two-year programs for technicians, four-year curricula for the bulk of scientists and engineers, and postgraduate programs of varying length for persons with higher aptitudes or interest in research. No such neat progression, however, has evolved or is likely to develop. The range of ability and special aptitudes in four-year engineering

[6] C. P. Snow, *The Two Cultures and the Scientific Revolution*, Cambridge University Press, New York, 1959, pp. 39–40.

schools is great, and students who earn degrees find diverse kinds and levels of jobs corresponding roughly, at least, with their abilities and educational attainments. Many are serving as little more than technicians. Others go into sales, supervisory, or managerial positions. A limited number with special aptitudes and, increasingly, with advanced training find their way ultimately into research, design, or development. Thus, in a fumbling, awkward way, with little conscious design, our higher institutions serve a wide variety of technical, semiprofessional, and professional occupations. Surely it ought to be possible to do this more effectively, with more efficient expenditure of funds, by a more rationally differentiated system and better placement of students. After studying the present and probable future need for technicians in relation to that for professional engineers, Henninger concluded that there is a current shortage of technicians and a current market for 30 per cent more engineering technicians than are available. He also found that within the next decade employers would prefer to hire twice as many new engineering technicians as new graduate engineers.

Henninger declared that the student who finishes the first two years of an accredited four-year engineering curriculum is not adequately prepared for productive employment as an engineering technician. He would have been more effectively trained for such employment, said Henninger, in a program more technical than the conventional engineering curriculum, yet emphasizing the understanding and practical application of basic science and mathematics rather than the proficiency in manual skills which is the mark of the trade school. Technical education, asserted Henninger, can be given better in two-year technical institutes and in well-established technical divisions of junior colleges than in four-year institutions.[7]

At the other end of the scale, at least a few engineering schools

[7] G. R. Henninger, *The Technical Institute in America*, McGraw-Hill Book Company, Inc., New York, 1959, p. 135.

are needed with selective admission, strong scientific and theoretical emphasis, a research orientation, and a graduate program
of high quality. The Massachusetts Institute of Technology and
the California Institute of Technology are the prototypes in private higher education. A few state university schools of engineering, especially in states where other public engineering schools
are available, might well emulate them.

TRAINING IN DEPTH
FOR AMERICAN CITIZENSHIP

In a democracy, training in depth is necessary not only in science and technology; it is equally essential in the humanities and
the social sciences if ordinary citizens are to follow in civic affairs
and in society generally the leadership of men of intelligence,
sensitivity, and idealism. Some years ago the writer tried to indicate the importance of this in speaking as follows at an interna-
tional conference of universities: [8]

All education in the United States, elementary, secondary,
and higher, is based on the belief that a democracy cannot
exist and grow merely through the leadership of an intellectual elite. The recent development of both secondary and
higher education in our country is an expression of the con-
viction that a modern democratic society must have a large
body of citizens who possess a deep understanding of the
problems of modern life; who are devoted to the purposes
and ideals of a free society; and who will take a responsible
and enlightened part in public affairs, both national and in-
ternational. Furthermore, there is a widespread feeling that
the highly educated few are unlikely to be recognized or accepted as leaders in a democracy if the great body of citizens

[8] *Report of Preparatory Conference of Representatives of Universities,*
United Nations Educational, Scientific, and Cultural Organization,
Paris, 1948, pp. 145-156.

have no basis of communication with them. The problems of human society are not likely to be solved as long as there exists a great intellectual gulf between the highly educated few and the meagerly educated masses. The differences among citizens in a democracy should take the form of gradations instead of sharp distinctions between the uninformed and the enlightened, the uncultured and the cultivated, the vocationally educated and the liberally educated man.

The subject of this excerpt, of course, was general or liberal education. The sharing of common knowledge and ideals through general education is a cohesive social force. General education should reduce provincialism and widen intellectual horizons; it should inspire devotion to the conditions of freedom and inculcate a sense of social and ethical obligation; it should emphasize a central intelligence which will integrate what one learns; it should release the humane sensibilities and aesthetic discernment of which the individual is capable. General education should enhance individuality. If it is meaningful, it should also engender respect for differences in talent and outlook among educated men.

Our society needs citizens who have had a generous liberal education—citizens whose formal college work has been largely in nonvocational studies. All whose formal education extends beyond the high school need some contact with the world of ideas, the life of the spirit, the world of beauty, the need for civic intelligence.

But although preparation in depth is essential for both specialized callings and general education, there is no reason to assume that both kinds of education must be attained in the same combination, the same order, the same way, or in the same institutions. They need not always be acquired in daytime schooling. Both general and specialized education may be continued over many years.

FLEXIBILITY IN TIME AND RELATIONSHIP

The organizational relationship between general and specialized education should be highly flexible. Traditionally, most of the first two years of a four-year college program are reserved for general education, and the last two for vocational, professional, or academic specialization. This may be appropriate for many students; for others, the Harvard plan, in which courses in general education are distributed throughout the four years, may be better; for still other students, it might be most fruitful to reverse the typical arrangement by letting them concentrate on their special interests in the early college years and to liberalize their programs at the end.

The last-mentioned scheme has been adopted at the Rochester Institute of Technology. The following excerpts from a recent catalogue suggest the institute's educational philosophy and curricular organization:

> It is known, first of all, that students learn most effectively when their learning experiences relate to their major interests. The Institute's plan of study capitalizes upon the particular interests of the student by providing him with technical and professional studies in his chosen field from the very beginning and continuing throughout his program. . . . Learning is most effective when it proceeds from the specific and concrete to the more general and abstract. The R.I.T. curriculums are designed to help the student integrate specific facts, observations, and experiences into broader and broader concepts.

This broadening carries over into general education, which is more fully represented in the final than in the first year of the student's program.

LIBERAL AND SPECIALIZED ADULT EDUCATION

Flexibility in the pursuit and combination of general and specialized education would do much to take the pressure off colleges and universities for physical expansion. The burden of mounting daytime enrollments in colleges and universities might be alleviated if students were encouraged to do their work in the late afternoon and evening. In the California state colleges, especially those in metropolitan areas, the late afternoon and evening programs, both in liberal arts and professions, which are designed mainly for "limited" students taking fewer than six semester hours of work, have been expanding more rapidly than the regular daytime courses. In 1950, 85 per cent of the state college students were "regular" students, but by 1958 the percentage had decreased to 65. Many of the part-time students are young adults.

Adult education is rapidly growing in this country. The number of adult part-time students in California grew from 226,280 to 417,433 beween 1947 and 1957. In the fall of 1957 adult part-time students outnumbered full-time day students in the California junior colleges two to one. A recent study showed that 6,600 adults were registered in evening classes conducted by the high schools, the public junior colleges, a state college, and the University of California in Contra Costa County, which is in the Bay area but which does not include either San Francisco or Berkeley, where the state college and the campus of the University of California are situated. Twenty-five hundred students were in the evening divisions of the two public junior colleges.

More than a third of the Contra Costa junior college adult students were high school graduates, and a tenth of them had college degrees. Four-fifths of the University of California extension students were high school graduates, and half of them held college degrees.

A short intelligence test was given to a sample of the 6,600 adults. Their average score was above that of 6,000 randomly selected high school seniors and equal to that of a sample of East Contra Costa Junior College freshmen.[9]

In his nation-wide study of junior colleges, Dr. Leland L. Medsker of the Center for the Study of Higher Education found that these institutions quickly become centers of attraction for adults. Adult classes are often scheduled during the day, and regular courses are sometimes scheduled at night, so that part-time students may take advantage of special courses or register for those regularly credited toward the associate degree. In a sample of thirty-seven junior colleges, Medsker found about 100,000 adults enrolled in credit and noncredit courses.[10]

In the study of 6,600 adult students in Contra Costa County, an attempt was made to find out why they had returned to school. When asked for the most important reason, 33 per cent stated interest in economic advancement, and 14 per cent interest in educational advancement, which often probably amounted to the same thing. This is the familiar economic motive which has been so prominent among adult students. It is an incentive not to be disparaged. The rapid changes in technology make better **education** in mathematics and the basic sciences, as well as in engineering applications, essential. Furthermore, at professional as well as subprofessional levels, new discoveries and developments make continuing education imperative. Continuing professional education in medicine, law, engineering, and other fields has expanded enormously. Thus, at the adult level, training in depth is essential —the range is from technical education to the most advanced professional specialties.

Adults may also extend, or even begin, their general and liberal education. In the California study, 14 per cent of the adult stu-

[9] C. E. Chapman, "Some Characteristics of Adult Part-time Students," *Adult Education*, vol. 10, pp. 27–41, Autumn, 1959.

[10] L. L. Medsker, *The Junior College: Progress and Prospect*, McGraw-Hill Book Company, Inc., New York, 1960, p. 74.

dents said their principal reason for taking courses was "to understand life better," "to learn more about the fine arts," "to enjoy the intellectual stimulation not found in the day-by-day experiences of life," "to know more, to broaden my horizons," or to satisfy some other cultural or intellectual interest.[11] In Medsker's sample of thirty-seven junior colleges, slightly more than half of the adult students were taking courses in language and communication, social science, fine and applied arts, mathematics, and natural science.[12] No information was given concerning the specific nature of these courses or the level at which they were given, but from this and other sources a definite trend toward adult general and liberal education is clearly apparent.

Pursuing general education *after* rather than *before* specialization may mean for many people postponing a part of it to the years after full-time schooling has ceased. Liberal studies may be most meaningful to adults who have assumed the full responsibilities of vocation and citizenship. Postponement may be dangerous, of course, unless the student acquires interests during college that will activate his desire for a fuller liberal education. For this reason, if for no other, every curriculum should make some place for general studies.

As continuing education becomes increasingly common, all sorts of arrangements of vocational and general, professional and liberal education will be possible. Much of what we assume should be learned by adolescents may be better acquired by adults. There is no reason why much of the load which formal, full-time education has normally carried cannot in the future become a part-time activity. Such rescheduling should enable us not so much to weave both vocational training and general education into a person's curriculum as to weave them into his life. And by keeping both kinds of education open at all levels, the education—and re-education—in depth that our society requires becomes possible.

[11] Chapman, *op. cit.*
[12] Medsker, *loc. cit.*

V DISTINCTIVENESS AND DIFFEREN-TIATION OR DUPLICATION?

The diversity of students' attributes and the multifarious demands of the American society for educated manpower would seem to call for a reasonable division of labor among higher institutions; yet colleges and universities tend to converge rather than to diverge, to become more similar and less differentiated.

The growing pressure by state governments for more systematic and coordinated development of public colleges and universities sharply raises the question of appropriate institutional roles. Any master plan for the state-wide development of higher education will inevitably provide for some differentiation of functions to make systematic what might otherwise be chaotic.

But attempts to allocate differential functions run against stubborn impediments. These center sometimes in the ambitions of the institutions themselves, sometimes in the students and parents who make little distinction between just going to college and going for a specific purpose or who, if they do make distinctions among institutions or educational programs, select the ones that conform to some stereotype of what "college" is.

THE "COLLEGE" STEREOTYPE

The Center for the Study of Higher Education has explored some of the demographic aspects of the functioning of higher education, including the relationship of certain factors to the percentages of college-age youths in college, state by state. One of the Center's hypotheses was that a positive relationship should exist between the range or diversity of educational offerings in a state's system of public higher education and the percentage of the age group actually in college. The data, however, did not support the hypothesis. This lack of relationship suggests that, in general, young people do not go to college for particular types of educational opportunity.[1] The numerous exceptions to this statement will come quickly to mind: many students enter undergraduate curricula in engineering, agriculture, business administration, and other occupational fields; others choose premedical or prelegal programs. Yet a very large number go to college simply because it is the thing to do and often enter particular curricula with little understanding of what they entail, where they lead, or what abilities they require.

TERMINAL JUNIOR COLLEGE CURRICULA LOSE THE BATTLE FOR STATUS

Many students select educational programs for the social or educational prestige they carry. This may be illustrated by the preference of junior college students for transfer over terminal programs. Presumably one of the unique purposes of the junior college is to prepare students for technical occupations or the semiprofessions and to offer a general education adapted to the

[1] J. G. Darley, *Distribution of Scholastic Ability in Higher Education*, unpublished manuscript, Center for the Study of Higher Education.

abilities of students who will not transfer to four-year institutions. However, in the course of a study of seventy junior colleges in fifteen states, conducted under the auspices of the Center, Medsker discovered that in many of these institutions terminal curricula do not exist, and in those where they do exist, often attract relatively few students. He found that in the fall of 1956 only a third of the students in the seventy junior colleges had enrolled in formal terminal programs or had chosen courses with an immediate vocational objective in mind. He also found that although two-thirds of the students were enrolled in transfer curricula, only one-third of the entrants in the fall of 1952 actually transferred to four-year institutions. These data are for all institutions together; there were wide variations from junior college to junior college. The technical courses in some community colleges or technical institutes carry high prestige in the community and show a large enrollment. Some of these curricula require a fairly extensive foundation in science and mathematics.[2] A survey of technical institutes conducted under the auspices of the American Society for Engineering Education listed forty-six junior colleges offering high-grade technical education.[3]

But in most comprehensive community colleges, the so-called "terminal" programs seem to wage a difficult and often a losing battle for status in competition with transfer curricula, which carry the prestige of corresponding to "real" college courses and of preparing students to go on "to college" in four-year institutions. The experience of New York State suggests that technical education develops most fully in an institution engaged solely in it. The New York State technical institutes were established to prepare students for well-defined technical occupations without reference to the possible transfer value of their courses. In prac-

[2] L. L. Medsker, *The Junior College: Progress and Prospect*, McGraw-Hill Book Company, Inc., New York, 1960, p. 74.

[3] G. R. Henninger, *The Technical Institute in America*, McGraw-Hill Book Company, Inc., New York, 1959, p. 135.

tice, four-year engineering schools have given varying amounts of credit for work done in the technical institutes, but this has been an incidental and not a primary consideration to the latter. In the fall of 1958 more than 90 per cent of the 14,023 students enrolled in New York's nineteen public two-year colleges, including the six state-supported agricultural and technical institutes were in terminal programs.[4] The strongest of the technical institutes have been amazingly successful in attracting capable students, in securing the cooperation and support of industry, and in placing their graduates. For example, the Erie County Technical Institute in Buffalo has enjoyed widespread respect in the community and has attracted students from a large area. Its curricula in building, electrical, industrial, chemical, mechanical, and metallurgical technology have been conducted at a high level, and its graduates have been in strong demand.

Recently most of the New York State technical institutes have been transformed into comprehensive community colleges offering preparatory as well as terminal curricula, and the master plan of the state university has recommended that with one exception all public two-year colleges should establish university-parallel programs in the arts and sciences.[5] No doubt the impetus that the basically nontransfer courses of the technical institutes have developed will carry these courses forward for some time. But the technical programs probably will gradually lose status and attraction in competition with transfer programs. Parents, students, and the community will tend to devalue what does not really mean "college" to them. Perhaps the New York technical institutes should become community colleges in the interest of wider service and a wider student body, but the popularity of terminal technical education will undoubtedly suffer from the transformation.

[4] Medsker, *op. cit.*, p. 117.
[5] *The Master Plan*, State University of New York, Albany, 1961.

PARENTS', STUDENTS', AND FACULTIES'
ATTITUDES IMPEDE DIVERSIFICATION

Students and parents often fail to perceive, or choose realistically from, the diversity of educational opportunities presumably available. Instead, they buy, so far as they can afford it, the education that approximates their own notions of quality and concepts of what education can do for them.
As Darley has said: [6]

> Higher education carefully refrains from publishing "consumers' guides"; parents and students are left to form their own standards of value to guide their investment. Institutional "halos" or institutional proximity, constrained by family resources, may be more powerful forces in attracting students than are the programs offered. The diversity of higher education, so real to educators, may be less clear to students and less accessible to them than we might think.

Faculty attitudes often are not conducive to real diversification. Dr. J. G. Darley, until recently associate dean of the Graduate School at the University of Minnesota, has pointed out that the graduate schools turn out future college faculty members whose image of the academic life converges toward a single standard of expectation rather than differential standards based on variation in student characteristics among different types of institutions. Darley has concluded: [7]

> Thus, it may be argued that a faculty's expectations of its own role, and that student and parental expectations for the outcomes of education conjoin to bring about a large measure of geographic duplication in higher education; but

[6] Darley, *op. cit.*
[7] *Ibid.*

duplication is not diversity. It is true . . . that student ability levels differ among types of institutions and within institutions. But diversity would also require that the processes of higher education be consciously geared to these differences and that the outcomes of the enterprise reflect these differences. The evidence for such adaptation is dubious, either in methods of instruction, planned differentiation of degree offerings, or clear awareness by teachers of student ability levels.

HIERARCHIES OF EDUCATIONAL
PRESTIGE AND VALUE

There seems to be a kind of "pecking order" of public prestige (and faculty valuation) among higher institutions. At this moment, with the prospect of soaring enrollments, many junior colleges probably desire to become four-year institutions. State colleges are changing their names to universities. (In many instances the change may be appropriate.) In these new universities the faculties are undoubtedly striving to approximate the educational values they associate with some stereotype, some standard of excellence or reputation. If the faculty of the preferred institution engages in research (or purports to do so), the aspiring faculty will press for time, facilities, and rewards for research. If the model multiplies courses and specializations, the ambitious institution will do the same, often at the cost of general educational enfeeblement. If the prototype has professional schools, the advancing institution will try to establish many of the same professional divisions, whether the state needs them or not. Thus we tend to have duplication, if only by a pale reflection of the model, rather than meaningful diversification.

THE IMITATION OF PRESTIGIOUS MODELS

Riesman has pointed out that any one clear or accepted scale—any single standard—for ranking American colleges and universities no longer exists; with great educational improvement on a nation-wide scale, no single institution can any longer dominate all others. The land-grant college or state university, for example, is not likely to look to an Ivy League university for a solution to its problems. While Riesman concludes that there is no single lighthouse, he admits that institutions do imitate each other, and the question is "which other?" Each college or university, depending on a realistic or fanciful notion of its stage of development, its limitations, and its possibilities, has its own model, its own image of quality, status, and prestige.

The recognition attained by land-grant colleges is said to be a refutation of the generalization that most institutions attempt to gain status by developing imitatively rather than distinctively. But separate land-grant colleges gained broad public acceptance painfully. For a long time they were called "cow colleges." They have managed to escape this appellation by becoming more like the state universities, and, as noted above, they have reached their maturity by graduating in name from "colleges" to "universities."

Not every state university is oblivious of the Ivy League, either. The University of California feels little affinity for the other state universities; it is unlikely to compare itself to any of them, with the possible exception of the University of Michigan. California's model is Harvard. In identifying itself with Harvard it is easy to forget at times that it is a land-grant institution. Some members of the faculty are probably only dimly aware that in some corners of the sprawling university are colleges of agriculture, an agricultural experiment station, an agricultural extension division, and several departments of home economics.

Riesman has illustrated the imitative tendency of American higher institutions by reflections on his experience, as a young graduate of the Harvard Law School, on the faculty of the Law School of the University of Buffalo.

Half the Buffalo law faculty members were Harvard trained. Most of these wanted to teach the courses which their Harvard experience had told them carried the greatest prestige—such as courses in labor law, constitutional law, and administrative law. Some of the members, including Riesman, thought the Buffalo Law School should not be a second-rate copy of Eastern models but should orient itself to the particular problems of its own area. But this, said Riesman, would have been interpreted as an intellectual defeat, "as having become provincial under the impact of local pressures, as a discredited vocationalism concerned with the State bar exams and the local job market." Thus, these faculty members could not carry their colleagues; the good students, together with most of their teachers, kept their eyes on the national scene and expressed little interest in the problems of western New York.[8]

Riesman had left the University of Buffalo before this writer arrived there as chancellor, but the attitude described was still endemic. The Law School faculty, with one or two exceptions, took little interest in the activities of the bar in the community; it expressed little concern with the problems of urbanization or local government; the local profession had little sense of identity with the Law School, or the school with the profession; the eyes of the faculty members were on the far horizon; the dean had just left to join the Harvard faculty; and one had the impression that others were waiting on the edges of their chairs for the call —from Harvard or some other law school that towered well above the province in which it was situated.

It is easy to oversimplify the imitative tendency in higher

[8] David Riesman, *Constraint and Variety in American Education*, University of Nebraska Press, Lincoln, 1956, pp. 29–30.

education. There are many systems or "leagues" among colleges and universities, each with its most prestigious models. Some institutions strain now and then to move from one system to another—from college to university status, for example. But often the greatest effort to approach an institutional standard of excellence or reputation is within a system or type. Many liberal arts colleges would like to become Swarthmores or Amhersts or whatever institutions seem to them to stand at the summit; if this goal is beyond the realm of possible attainment, they may lower their sights to a star not so high in the firmament. Yet there are liberal arts colleges which seem to get more satisfaction from taking on some of the specialized trappings of a state college or university—such as courses in business administration, medical technology, or nursing—than from striving for greater excellence in basic liberal studies. Most state colleges, including those which were previously teachers colleges, are ambitious for university status.

CALIFORNIA'S EFFORT FOR INSTITUTIONAL
DIFFERENTIATION

Although California is in some ways atypical in higher education, many of the impediments to the development of institutional differentiation can be illustrated there. In this state an attempt has been made, with only limited success, to maintain a tripartite, differentiated system of public higher education composed of the University of California, the state colleges, and the junior colleges. Two surveys of the state's needs in higher education, one published in 1948 and the other in 1955, recommended that the three groups of institutions should perform some common and some differential functions.[9] Both reports recognized that the

[9] M. E. Deutsch, A. A. Douglas, and G. D. Strayer, *A Report of a Survey of the Needs of California in Higher Education*, University of California Press, Berkeley, Calif., 1948. T. C. Holy, T. R. McConnell,

state colleges, as well as the university, should offer strong programs of general and liberal education and that the junior colleges should provide transfer curricula preparatory to upper-division work in four-year institutions. They agreed that both the state colleges and the university should prepare teachers but that the former should continue to emphasize teacher education as their primary function. The surveys also took note of the development of four-year curricula in the state colleges and the university in some of the same vocational fields—engineering, agriculture, business administration, and public administration, for example.

The 1948 survey attempted, however, to work out a plan of differential functions among the three groups of institutions. Thus it proposed that the junior colleges take special responsibility for technical curricula, the state colleges for "occupational" curricula, and the University of California for graduate and professional education and research. The 1955 survey—the Restudy—recommended that this division of responsibility be continued.[10]

The Restudy found it difficult, however, to make clear distinctions between "occupational" and "professional" curricula in such fields as business administration and public administration. It concluded that differentiation of function may be mainly one of emphasis on the theoretical or the practical, the fundamental or the applied; that the differentiation should be primarily one of level, with certain institutions offering two-year curricula, others confining their offerings to four-year undergraduate programs or five-year curricula, and the university concentrating

and H. H. Semans, *A Restudy of the Needs of California in Higher Education,* California State Department of Education, Sacramento, 1955.

[10] The word "occupational" was obviously a makeshift term. It was defined in the 1948 report as the "level between the *technical* training of the junior college and the *professional* and research departments of the University towards which the *occupational* curricula of the state colleges are pointed."

on graduate curricula leading to the doctorate, on the higher professions, and on research. The Restudy also proposed that under certain conditions the state colleges should award the master's degree both in applied fields and in the liberal arts.

DIFFERENTIAL FUNCTIONS
IN ENGINEERING EDUCATION

Some time before the Restudy report, the state colleges and the university had entered into an agreement on engineering education which attempted to stake out the respective differential responsibilities of the two types of institutions. Subsequently, in the light of this agreement a report was prepared which assigned to the university responsibility for the more theoretical curricula stressing design, research, and development, and to the state colleges the more practical educational programs leading to positions in production, construction, operation, application, sales, and service.

Because, as a consequence, their graduates could not attain state licenses as professional engineers, it was unfortunate that the engineering agreement specified that the state colleges should not attempt to secure accreditation of their engineering curricula by the Engineering Council for Professional Development. The agreement also limited the colleges to undergraduate programs. Under pressure by the state colleges and by industry, particularly in the area around San Jose and the San Francisco Bay, both these restrictions have since been removed.

That the distinction between the engineering functions of design, research, and development and those of production, operation, and sales is not arbitrary was confirmed later, independently, by an analysis of the activities in which engineers engaged in five large corporations. In a study conducted by the Educational Testing Service, a factor analysis of the tasks which engineers performed in these companies yielded five principal, partly overlapping clusters of activities. One of these clusters seemed to be uniquely important in jobs commonly called "research" and of considerable importance in those known as "development" or "product improvement." The second cluster represented emphasis on "development," "production," and "sales." The third cluster included activities supporting technical services. The fourth had to do predominantly with "design," and the last with "supervision" and possibly "administration." [11] This functional classification is similar to that used in the report on differential responsibilities of the state colleges and the University of California.

Not only do discriminable engineering functions seem to exist that cut across conventional engineering curricula, but there is also some evidence that the people performing different functions differ in personal characteristics. For example, engineers engaged in research and development have higher scores on measures of inductive reasoning and interest in ideas; they are more self-critical; and they have a tendency to make remote rather than obvious, uncommon rather than frequent, and clever rather than banal, responses on an "idea classification" test.[12]

Students with actual or potential characteristics comparable to those of engineers engaged in research and design are probably in limited supply. Furthermore, faculty members qualified to staff an educational program emphasizing these aspects of engineering are even less numerous. It seems reasonable, therefore, to attempt to concentrate the students and the faculty, together with the relevant teaching and research facilities, in a limited number of centers.

[11] D. R. Saunders, *Objective Description and Classification of Engineering Jobs, II: Factor Analysis of the Key Group Data Form,* Educational Testing Service, Research Bulletin, Princeton, April, 1956.

[12] D. R. Saunders, "Some Measures Related to Success and Placement in Basic Engineering Research and Development," in C. Taylor (ed.), *1955 University of Utah Research Conference on the Identification of Creative Scientific Talent,* University of Utah Press, Salt Lake City, 1956.

But in the academic, if not in the industrial, world, the symbols of prestige are attached to research and design rather than to sales and production, the more "practical" aspects of engineering. The proposal to give training emphasizing the former phases of engineering to the University of California only enhanced their valuation; this allocation thus seemed to favor the university over the state colleges. Consequently, at least some of the colleges, struggling against the "fetters," strove to make their engineering curricula more, rather than less, like those of the university.

INSTITUTIONAL DIFFERENTIATION
IN AGRICULTURE

In agriculture, a somewhat different attitude exists between the University of California at Davis and at least one of the state colleges. A recent study showed that the two institutions profess different educational objectives: California State Polytechnic College, it is said, emphasizes the "know-how" of agricultural production and learning by doing through individual projects; Davis places its emphasis on theoretical training based on scientific principles. In general, the faculties of the two institutions supported these broad purposes in the investigation in question, but there was some divergence in point of view in each institution. At California Polytechnic, a younger faculty group wished to rewrite the curriculum to meet the needs of a more diversified student body and to provide a stronger scientific foundation. At Davis, on the other hand, a group believed that the scientific emphasis can be carried too far and that the University of California should appeal to a larger segment of California youth.

The curricula and the student programs in the agricultural fields studied reflected the differences in objectives. California Polytechnic required that half of the student's program be in applied agriculture; Davis required a quarter. Davis required that a third of the student's program be given to the supporting sciences; California Polytechnic required only a fifth of the student's time in the basic disciplines.

Were there differences in the characteristics of the students in the two institutions corresponding to the distinction in objectives and curriculum? The study gave a qualified negative answer to this question. The two student bodies differed in general scholastic aptitude,[13] and a higher percentage of Davis freshmen had high scores on the scientific keys of the Strong Vocational Interest Blank, but the differences, although statistically significant, were small. These differences were not in the direction that would be predicted if the differential objectives were functionally effective in attracting students. It was Davis rather than the state college which had a higher percentage of students with interest patterns in technical and business fields. One would have expected the difference to be in the other direction.

If the institutions and student bodies were relevantly paired, one would expect the Davis students to be significantly higher on measures of complexity of outlook, originality, and interest in ideas as ideas, which in the Center's studies have been found to be associated with a theoretical disposition. Surprisingly, the two student bodies were not significantly different in these regards. The scores on other measures of personality did show a greater concern for social responsibility and a less authoritarian attitude among the Davis students.

There were some differences in the students' appraisal of the institutions and in their own educational values. The Davis students stated that they had chosen the institution because of its academic reputation or because of the excellence of its training. They said they believed that a satisfying career should give them

[13] The requirements for admission at Davis are much higher than at the other institution. Agricultural students in the university, with minor exceptions, have to meet the same scholastic standards and present the same pattern of high school courses for admission as other students.

the opportunity to use their special abilities. In contrast, the California Polytechnic students declared that they had chosen the college because of its emphasis on the applied method of teaching. They believed that a satisfying career should provide a stable, secure future.

Finally, it was found that the jobs which the alumni of the two institutions held immediately after graduation did not differ significantly. The occupational data were secured in January, 1958, from graduates of 1955 and 1956. Perhaps as time goes on the careers of the two groups of graduates will diverge.

One must conclude, as the author of the study did, that, with the exception of the principal reasons students gave for choosing the one institution or the other, neither prospective students nor employers perceived the differences in objectives and educational programs; or else that students' choices were more influenced by other factors, such as geographical proximity, than by the nature of the institutions themselves.

In spite of the present differences in the educational characteristics of the two schools, both increasingly desire students who have the interests, aptitudes, and academic background to complete undergraduate programs that will qualify them to be agriculture teachers, plant and sales managers in "agri-business," and graduate students and research workers in agricultural colleges and universities. As noted above, some of the California Polytechnic faculty would like to make that college more like Davis. This is not surprising, because most of them have had their graduate training in institutions with an orientation different from the one in which they are now teaching. Apparently the Davis faculty lacks the courage of the university's convictions: it has introduced a curriculum in agricultural production, which has been the other institution's forte. This is but another example of the tendency toward duplication rather than diversity, toward convergence rather than distinctiveness.

These considerations led the author of the mentioned study to observe that diversity could be attained through flexible programs in a single institution as well as by different programs in two or more places, provided the single institution made possible and encouraged a high degree of curricular and instructional individualization. He also pointed out that if a single institution could meet the needs of desirable diversification and take care of enough students, the high cost of agricultural education would make duplication of curricula and preparation of students for the same types of positions in two or more institutions unjustifiable. In this connection, he reported that with an undergraduate agricultural enrollment of 539 men in the fall of 1957 at the University of California, its outstanding facilities for agricultural education were far from being overloaded; without the prospect of a general increase in agricultural enrollments, he found it difficult to see the need for the great number of places for students in agricultural programs now being offered by twenty-eight junior colleges, four state colleges, and three campuses of the university.[14]

Yet the University of California is highly selective and has adopted the policy of establishing comparable standards of admission throughout; it would therefore probably not wish to admit students in its agricultural divisions with lesser academic ability than students in other parts of the university, particularly since the university's agricultural colleges are now parts of more general campuses.

A BASIC DIVISION OF RESPONSIBILITY

If instruction in agriculture and engineering is to be distributed among several institutions, it seems theoretically sound to allocate

[14] E. D. Farwell, "Diversification in Undergraduate Agricultural Education in Selected Institutions," unpublished doctoral dissertation, University of California, Berkeley, 1959.

specialized curricula in scientific and theoretical agriculture or in engineering research and design to particular institutions, if only for the reason that students with the necessary abilities and intellectual dispositions are not numerous. Yet the California experience suggests that such allocation will be difficult to attain in practice; one reason is that in choosing institutions the students do not distribute themselves appropriately. What minimum division of responsibility among the institutions of a state-wide system may we then expect?

In agriculture and engineering, one may ask in the interests of economy and quality, at least, that no more agricultural and engineering schools or divisions be established than a state really needs. A general principle to be observed in placing institutions and distributing educational programs in a state-wide system of higher education is that the most general kinds of education—those that serve the greatest number of students—should be widely dispersed and the most specialized programs—those that enroll few students—concentrated in a single institution or in a very limited number of places.

This principle suggests that junior college education should be widely available geographically. Four-year curricula in the liberal arts, whether in separate colleges or in complex institutions, might also be regionally dispersed, but not as widely as junior colleges. Since some professional or subprofessional curricula attract a large number of students, they, too, may be allocated to a number of institutions. Perhaps teacher education, traditionally available in liberal arts colleges as well as in special teacher-training colleges, should be offered at most four-year institutions. Business administration could be justified at fewer places. A still smaller number of institutions would need to offer engineering and social work. Finally, legal and medical education in the public system should be a monopoly of a single state university in most states. As to graduate education, most four-year institutions should be content to offer only the baccalaureate degree; those offering the master's might be somewhat more numerous; and those awarding the doctorate should be small in number if the degree is not to be debased. In most states, this will mean no more than two public institutions will offer the doctorate—the state university and the land-grant university—and between these two, allocation of many specialties will be necessary if educational debility is to be avoided. This may seem too severe; yet for numerous institutions to give doctoral degrees in many fields would strain available financial resources and sound educational standards. This was the attitude taken in a recent survey of higher education in Michigan, which stated that even in such fields as educational administration, in which they might appropriately offer two-year graduate programs, the state-colleges-turned-universities should not give doctoral degrees for some time to come.[15]

There has recently been strong pressure by the California state colleges to give doctoral degrees. In 1955 the *Restudy of the Needs of California in Higher Education* recommended that "at least until 1965, and also after 1965, unless new and compelling factors arise that cannot now be anticipated, degrees at the doctoral level in publicly supported institutions be awarded exclusively by the University of California." This recommendation was officially approved by the governing boards of the university and the state colleges. Nevertheless, by 1959 some of the state colleges were demanding the right to award doctoral degrees, although no compelling need was demonstrated. The ensuing controversy led to the governor's demand that the state colleges and university come forward with plans to coordinate their activities and to a legislative resolution directing the Liaison Committee [16] of the Regents of the University and the State

[15] J. D. Russell, *Higher Education in Michigan,* Michigan Legislative Study Committee on Higher Education, Lansing, 1958, p. 147.

[16] This was a voluntary coordinating body composed of the chief executive officer and four members each from the Regents of the University of California and the State Board of Education.

Board of Education (which governed the state colleges) to prepare a master plan for meeting California's educational needs
during the next ten years.

The master plan subsequently agreed upon by both governing boards and submitted to the Legislature in December, 1959,
stated that "the University shall have the sole authority in public
higher education to award the doctor's degree in all fields of
learning, *except that* it may agree with the state colleges to award
joint doctor's degrees in selected fields."

Not only are there to be cooperative doctoral programs, but
the university and state college concerned are to confer the degree
jointly. This differs from the arrangement that has been in effect
for some time in Ohio whereby work taken under certain conditions at the other state universities may be applied toward the
doctorate at the Ohio State University. (Ohio University at
Athens has recently inaugurated a Ph.D. program.) Presumably,
however, the University of California will be able to determine
in what fields the joint arrangement may be made and will be in
a position to control the standards under which the degree will
be awarded. These and other issues under the new plan remain to
be resolved. Little will have been accomplished if the scheme
results in the proliferation of graduate courses and joint degrees
in fields where no such expansion is needed. Something constructive may emerge if the present and future resources of both
systems are used to complement and supplement, rather than
duplicate, each other. If a careful design is not made in advance,
the state colleges may strain for staff and facilities in fields of
their own choosing, followed by demands on the university for
joint degrees. The past suggests that this is probable.

Some of the obstacles to the attainment of planned diversity
among the public higher institutions of a state have been suggested. Many students choose institutions or educational programs that conform to some stereotype of what "college" is. Both

students and parents often fail to perceive the spectrum of educational opportunities that lies before them, or, if they are aware of diverse offerings, they wish to embrace those that carry higher social or educational prestige. When students choose institutions, they tend to favor those on which their friends or certain social groups place higher valuation. These social forces make it difficult for an institution to develop a deviant role—one which would distinguish it from other colleges or give it a special character. There are exceptions, of course. Colleges like Sarah Lawrence and Bennington made capital out of being "experimental" (while appealing to a well-to-do clientele). Antioch has attained a special status with its work-study program, although the public may perceive the purpose and value of the work experience differently from the way in which the faculty thinks of it. But all these institutions have somehow managed to remain in the public's mind as being in the general category of outstanding liberal arts colleges.

CORRELATES OF ACADEMIC STATUS

Many of the correlates of status in the academic world are well known. A junior college perceived as an upward extension of the high school and organizationally a part of a unified school system and school administration is likely to have less status than one which is set off from the high school in an autonomous district with a separate administration. The A.A. degree confers little status, the A.B. carries much more, the A.M. adds a definite increment, and the Ph.D. or an advanced professional degree represents the highest station. The institution which confers the highest degrees enjoys corresponding eminence. An institution whose roster of professional schools is limited to the so-called newer professions has less distinction than the one which confers degrees in law and medicine. Status will accrue to colleges in relation to the level of their curricula and to the status of the occupations for which they prepare.[17]

The public is not always aware of all these gradations; a faculty is especially sensitive to them. For this reason it is difficult to get institutions to accept, much less enthusiastically to espouse, differential roles if these roles deviate from the faculty's expectations of academic status. In these circumstances, to be different means to be inferior. Hence institutions strive to simulate whatever institution is far enough ahead to serve as a model. Sometimes this striving is clearly for excellence in either a current or a different role. At other times the striving is for a different form rather than a higher quality. Thus a teachers-college-turned-state-college, or, by name, university, may wish to copy a mediocre complex state university with numerous, if weak, schools and specialized departments rather than to become a strong liberal arts institution with few professional schools or curricula, and those securely anchored in the basic disciplines.

The faculty council of one of the California state colleges has expressed resentment over the attempt to differentiate the functions of three groups of higher institutions in that state. It asserted that the principle of differentiation seemed to mean that the university should offer a first-rate, the state colleges a second-rate, and the junior colleges a third-rate, education. The feeling that the state colleges had been assigned an inferior status arose from various sources, including the policy of making the University of California highly selective and the state colleges less so, and the proposal that the state colleges should offer "occupational" curricula in the lesser professions or curricula of a more practical sort than the university.

[17] For a fuller exposition of the factors related to institutional status, with particular reference to the position of the junior college, see B. R. Clark, *The Open Door College: A Case Study*, McGraw-Hill Book Company, Inc., New York, 1960, pp. 168–176.

AN INSTITUTIONAL HIERARCHY

In a public system of higher education capped by a selective university limited to special functions, there will be a hierarchy of institutions according to student ability. This occurs in other states than California. The Michigan report on higher education, for example, recommended that the University of Michigan should continue to place its chief emphasis on graduate and professional study and research of high quality, with a relatively limited freshman class of high ability. At the same time, the report proposed that Eastern Michigan College, which is situated near the university, should not attempt to attain university status and should not become an institution of highly selective character.[18]

If the trend toward greater selectivity by the major state universities continues, differences among the types of public institutions in a state may be accentuated. Differential selection will be reflected in progressive increases in average scholastic ability from the "lowest" to the "highest" institutions in the system. The junior colleges are likely to have the lowest average and widest range of ability to cope with (although there will be exceptions to this rank), and the university will serve the narrowest range and highest level of talent. But this does not mean that any group of institutions will get only the culls. All institutions in the hierarchy will have students of superior and outstanding talent, although some of them will admit *only* superior students.

A SINGLE STANDARD?

The state college faculty which protested against the policy of differential functions among the three segments of public

[18] Russell, *op. cit.*, pp. 144–145.

higher education in California as relegating the state colleges
to second-class academic status insisted that there should be more
rather than less duplication and that control over the development of the state colleges should be replaced by free competition.
It proposed that all public institutions in the state should be permitted to compete freely with one another in a continuing effort
to provide better programs of instruction.

Although this writer has been presenting the case for division
of labor in higher education, it is necessary to admit that the
consequences of straining to approximate a model or the consequences of competing for academic status are not always undesirable. Riesman has concluded that the gulf which once sep-
arated the most distinguished from the ordinary institutions has
narrowed greatly in recent years and that a hundred institutions
or more are in pursuit of the foremost ones.[19] Yet in spite of his
notion that the University of Buffalo Law School should identify
itself with its own region instead of imitating the national law
schools, and in spite of his observation that each institution tends
to compete in its own orbit, Riesman implied repeatedly that all
collegiate institutions should be evaluated by a single standard of
quality.

If we are to judge institutions by a single standard, it should
be the one proposed by Dr. John Gardner, who has declared that
we cannot hope to create or maintain an adequately diversified
system of higher education unless we "recognize that each of
the different kinds of institutions has its significant part to play
in creating the total pattern, and that each should be allowed to
play its role with honor and recognition." He added that "we
must develop a point of view that permits each kind of institution
to achieve excellence *in terms of its own objectives.*" [20] There is
no implication here that if an institution exists it *ipso facto* has

---

[19] Riesman, *op. cit.*, pp. 42–44.
[20] J. Gardner, *Excellence*, Harper & Brothers, New York, 1961, pp.
83, 84.

a significant role and that it is playing the part effectively. Neither is there any denial of the importance of standards. The statement is simply that institutions are to be judged by standards appropriate to their roles.

But it is easier to propose a point of view that permits each kind of institution to achieve excellence in terms of standards appropriate to its role than to explain how this is to be done. Both public and academic attitudes and expectations make it inordinately difficult. The problem of finding social supports for institutions of different types in a differentiated system has yet to be solved. Institutional autonomy is one of the supports that sociologists have identified,[21] and the significance of autonomy is clearly reflected in the state college faculty's plea for complete freedom to compete with other institutions, especially the universities. But no state is likely to provide the resources for turning many of its public institutions into first-class universities. The pressures for comprehensive planning of higher education in many states will result in some degree of patterning of public institutions—the organization of an articulated system. This will be accompanied by some loss of freedom of action. The pressing problem is how to leave particular institutions room for initiative, experimentation, and striving for excellence while they play their appropriate roles in the general plan.

[21] Clark, *op. cit.*, pp. 174–176.

VI THE PRIMACY OF THE UNIVERSITY

Implicit in the policy of differentiating the roles of public colleges and universities is the assumption that a democratic system of higher education need not accord all students the privilege of attending the same kinds of institutions, any more than it need permit all to pursue the same curricula.

A RADICAL REDISTRIBUTION OF STUDENTS

Dr. Conant has insisted on many occasions that a large part of the future enrollment in higher education should be accommodated in junior colleges, in fact, that there would be no inconsistency with our ideal of equal educational opportunity if these institutions were to enroll half the total number of college students. In this fashion, he said, the distribution of students among the several types of higher institutions could be radically altered without reducing the percentage of youths going on beyond the high school. One of the principal purposes of this redistribution would be to permit the major universites to concentrate on their proper role as centers of scholarly work, graduate and professional education, and research.[1]

MANY STATE UNIVERSITIES NOT
SUFFICIENTLY SELECTIVE

If a university is to be, as the dictionary defines it, an "institution of the highest grade," its enrollment should be limited to students capable of high achievement in the arts and sciences, and in professional and graduate studies. Yet in the country at large, the complex universities are only a little more selective than other types of institutions.

In its study of the selectivity of American higher education, the Center for the Study of Higher Education grouped the institutions in its representative national sample into two-year colleges, four-year institutions giving only the baccalaureate degree, institutions giving the first professional and first graduate degrees, and universities giving advanced professional and doctoral degrees. The mean academic aptitude test scores of the freshmen of 1952 in these four types of institutions were 94, 102, 106, and 113. The mean of all freshmen in the total sample was 104, and about two-thirds of the scores fell between 77 and 131. The mean of the public universities was 109 and of the private ones, 121. By 1959, in 167 of the 200 institutions in the 1952 national sample, the average of all freshmen had risen to 109. The mean of the public universities was 112; the range of institutional means was from 104 to 124. This represents a lesser degree of selection than one would desire in institutions which presumably make up the capstone of the American system of public higher education.

[1] J. B. Conant, *The Citadel of Learning,* Yale University Press, New Haven, Conn., 1956, pp. 70–71.

POOR SELECTION LEADS TO POOR RETENTION

It is not surprising that attrition in the major universities is high. Iffert found that about 43 per cent of the students who entered universities dropped out with no record of transfer to another institution. He estimated that about 60 per cent of the entrants ultimately graduated either from the university of first registration or from another institution.[2]

Detailed data on retention are available at the Center for most of the collegiate institutions in Minnesota, including the university. Survival in the University of Minnesota varies from division to division. Some of the university's schools and colleges have become more selective than the institution as a whole by declining to admit students of limited academic ability, who, however, may be accepted by the two-year General College of the university. Two of the most selective undergraduate divisions are the College of Science, Literature, and the Arts, and the Institute of Technology. In 1952, 61 per cent of the freshmen in the former and 70 per cent in the latter came from the top quarter of high school graduates.[3] Yet in the College of Science, Literature, and the Arts, only 56 per cent of the men and 45 per cent of the women had earned degrees or were still in school four years later. In the Institute of Technology, the corresponding percentage (men only) was 55. Thus, in an institution with some of the most selective undergraduate divisions in state universities, the attrition was still high.[4] In comparison with British universities it was exceedingly high. For example, among the stu-

[2] R. E. Iffert, *Retention and Withdrawal of College Students*, U.S. Office of Education Bulletin, no. 1, 1958.

[3] A recent study shows the mean ACE score of College of Science, Literature, and the Arts freshmen was slightly lower in 1958 than in 1952. R. F. Berdie et al., "Who Goes to College? Minnesota College Freshmen: A Comparison, 1930–1958," University of Minnesota Press, Minneapolis, (in press).

dents who entered the University of Liverpool in the three-year period 1947 to 1949, approximately 79 per cent of those in the Faculty of Arts and about 85 per cent of those in the Faculty of Engineering earned degrees in the normal time. Counting those who earned delayed degrees, more than 91 per cent of the entrants in each faculty were graduated.[5] It should be kept in mind that at entrance the English universities are much more selective than American state universities.

Not all who drop out along the way in American universities have unsatisfactory records or low ability. For example, in the Minnesota state colleges, the average high school percentile rank [6] of the men who had earned degrees or were still in school four years after admission in 1952 was only three points higher than that of the men who withdrew. (Those who had been officially dropped for low scholarship were excluded.) At the University of Minnesota, the average high school percentile rank of the men who earned degrees or were still in residence in the College of Science, Literature, and the Arts was 77; that of the men who withdrew was 71. Obviously, there were potentially capable students who dropped out, and some of them without question met at least the minimum standard for normal academic progress.[7]

It is always difficult to discover the real reasons, apart from low scholarship, for withdrawal or transfer. But there can be no doubt that incongruity, not only between aptitude and ability, but also between students' interests, motivations, personality characteristics, and the goals and demands of university cur-

[4] J. G. Darley, *Distribution of Scholastic Ability in Higher Education*, Center for the Study of Higher Education, University of California, Berkeley.

[5] Sir James Mountford, *How They Fared: A Survey of a Three-year Entry*, Liverpool University Press, Liverpool, 1957.

[6] This measure of ability has been one of the best predictors of academic success at the University of Minnesota.

[7] Darley, *op. cit.*

ricula, is one of the important factors. How much discrepancy the student can tolerate between his personal needs and purposes and the pressure of the institution is not yet known, but that in individual cases it reaches the breaking point has been demonstrated.[8]

SELECTION AFTER ADMISSION

It is often said that in the United States much of the selection for higher education takes place after, rather than before, admission. One would expect, therefore, to find that the graduates of the state universities would be very much higher in ability, on the average, than the freshman classes of which they were members. But, as the comparison between those who survived and those who withdrew suggests, the difference in ability between freshmen and graduates is not as great as one might suppose.

Although the Minnesota study showed that many capable students withdrew, the average ability of those who failed scholastically was very much lower than the average ability of those who survived or withdrew. But the average ability of those who earned degrees was not much higher than that of the entire freshman class. Here are some examples.

The average high school percentile rank of freshmen of 1952 in the four Minnesota state colleges was 50.8 for men and 67.1 for women. The average ranks of those who had earned degrees or were still in school four years later were 56.5 and 70.7. The freshman-senior differences in seven Minnesota four-year liberal arts colleges were somewhat greater: the freshman averages were 62.8 and 79.3; those of the survivors, 71.2 and 85.1. The freshman averages in the College of Science, Literature, and the Arts of the University of Minnesota for men and women were 68.8

[8] See G. G. Stern, M. I. Stein, and B. S. Bloom, *Methods in Personality Assessment*, Free Press, Glencoe, Ill. 1956.

and 81.8; of those who earned degrees or were still in school four
years later, 73 and 63. (This shows an enormous loss of capable
women, although some of them undoubtedly continued their
education elsewhere; the average rank of the women who withdrew was 95.) It is significant to note, also, that the variation in
the freshman and surviving groups was not greatly different.
That is, heterogeneity was characteristic of both.

One might conclude, therefore, that there is less selection, in
terms of initial ability at least, *after* admission to colleges and
universities than most observers have thought. The significant
point is, however, that the institutions' postadmission selective
processes search out not only ability but also other personal characteristics related to achievement and persistence, such as interest
and motivation. In the future it may be desirable to take these
factors into account in admitting students or, at least, in encouraging or discouraging them to enter. Work under way at the
Center for the Study of Higher Education gives promise of discovering how this might be done more effectively than it could
be managed at present.

POOR SELECTION DISTORTS PUBLIC IMAGE
OF THE UNIVERSITY

The enrollment of students who have little chance of completing requirements for degrees diverts the university from its
primary functions as university and distorts its image in the
public mind. The public may come to think of the university
at worst as a great undergraduate adolescent playground or as
a place where many can at least stay long enough to sample the
social pleasures of campus life, or at best as a place offering something for everybody from a two-year course in business practice
to advanced courses for M.D. and Ph.D. degrees. (The public

usually has little comprehension of what the latter entail; in fact, it often has no conception of the university as a place *primarily* engaged in serious intellectual effort.)

The functions of one of the most selective state universities have been defined as:[9]

1. Research directed toward advancing the understanding of the natural world and the interpretation of human history and of the great creations of humane insight and imagination.

2. Instruction of able young people; not merely by transmitting to them established knowledge and skills, but by helping them to experience with their teachers the actual processes of developing and testing new hypotheses and fresh interpretations in many fields.

3. Training for professional careers—a training not merely routine, but grounded in understanding of relevant sciences and literatures, and enlightened by some experience of the methods by which the boundaries of knowledge are pushed back.

4. Various sorts of expert public service.

A university pursuing these purposes, no matter how imperfectly they may be attained, requires students who possess not only superior academic ability but also serious intellectual interests. It is not surprising that only 15 per cent of the high school graduates of the state have recently been eligible for admission to this institution. It is not surprising either that a superior high school record or a superior score on a test of academic aptitude does not always signify serious intellectual interests or strong educational motivation. Consequently, attrition

[9] T. C. Holy, T. R. McConnell, and H. H. Semans, *A Restudy of the Needs of California in Higher Education,* California State Department of Education, Sacramento, 1955, p. 74.

at the university is substantial, although it is lower than at less selective institutions.[10] Furthermore, this university has more undergraduates in the upper division than in the freshman and sophomore years; it has become essentially an institution for advanced undergraduate, professional, and graduate study. In contrast, many state universities, particularly those in large urban communities, serve as great junior colleges, sifting from a large and heterogeneous mass the much smaller number of students who meet the institutions' requirements for graduation or admission to a professional school. It would be more relevant for these universities to concentrate their energies on the activities appropriate to a community of scholars.

The rapid development of other four-year public colleges into multipurpose institutions and the possibility of expanding the junior college system in many states have made it feasible for the principal state universities to (1) *recognize research both in the basic disciplines and in the professions as a primary function;* (2) *confine their educational programs primarily to advanced undergraduate, graduate, and professional fields, with strong emphasis on scholarly and theoretical foundations; and* (3) *admit only students thought to be capable of a high level of intellectual attainment.*[11]

To many members of the National Association of State Universities and of the American Association of Land-Grant Colleges and State Universities, certainly to many of the great leaders of the past, this proposal would repudiate the very foundations on which the state universities have risen. Cornell University was founded as "an institution in which any person can find instruc-

---

[10] One study showed that of 1,422 "native entering students" on one of the major campuses of the university, 62 per cent finished eight semesters on that or another campus of the university. This survival rate is still low in comparison with British universities.

[11] This emphasis on the university's academic program is not meant to preclude the expert service which has been traditional for the state universities and land-grant colleges to perform.

tion in any study." Under William Watts Folwell the University of Minnesota espoused the same philosophy.[12] There was in Minneapolis,

> as at Ithaca, the same devotion to the "all-purpose" curriculum, "embracing potentially all subjects of human and practical interest"; the same emphasis on equality of subjects; the same belief in the value of scientific research; the same concern with service to the needs of society through the systematic study of commerce, government and human relations.

"NO INTELLECTUAL SERVICE TOO UNDIGNIFIED TO PERFORM"

Lotus D. Coffman, also one of Minnesota's distinguished presidents, gave such eloquent voice to this attitude that he is quoted here at length:[13]

> The state universities hold that there is no intellectual service too undignified for them to perform. They maintain that every time they lift the intellectual level of any class or group, they enhance the intellectual opportunities of every other class or group. They maintain that every time they teach any group or class the importance of relying on tested information as the basis for action, they advance the cause of science. They maintain that every time they teach any class or group in society how to live better, to read more and to read more discriminatingly, to do any of the things which stimulate intellectual or aesthetic interest and effort, they thereby enlarge the group's outlook on life, make its members more cosmopolitan in their points of view, and

[12] J. S. Brubacher and W. Rudy, *Higher Education in Transition*, Harper & Brothers, New York, 1958, p. 161.
[13] L. D. Coffman, *The State University: Its Work and Problems*, copyright 1934 by the University of Minnesota, pp. 205–206.

improve their standard of living. Such services as these the state universities would not shrink from performing—indeed, would seek to perform.

Coffman was strongly opposed to the notion that the state universities should exist for an elite group, even for an intellectual elite. He said:[14]

> If college education is to be only for the select, then it becomes alien to the spirit which gave birth to public education and the state universities. . . . Let the state universities set themselves up as class institutions and the support which they have received hitherto will quickly vanish and out of the soil which gave them birth other institutions will rise to take their places.

"THE RIGHT TO TRY"

Coffman encouraged at his university and in his state a widespread testing program on the basis of which students could be counseled (before and after admission to the university) concerning their chances of academic success, the fields of study and the vocations for which they were best fitted. But he was opposed to arbitrary exclusion. The democratic method of guidance, he said, "recognizes that human judgment may err, that statistics may lie. Above all, it recognizes that great American principle— the right to try—knowing full well that industry sometimes succeeds even when high intelligence is wanting. . . . The thing about it all that appeals to me is that we have here a democratic method, a democratic experiment in democracy, if you please, that does not close the doors of opportunity to the aspiring slow students but encourages those of greater talents to seek training for leadership in increasing numbers." [15]

Two state universities have recently adduced evidence and

[14] *Ibid.*, pp. 42, 47.
[15] *Ibid.*, p. 139.

argument for Coffman's position. A study of the number of graduates in two undergraduate colleges of the University of Minnesota who would have been excluded had higher standards of admission been established for freshmen showed that it is possible to establish admission requirements that will exclude most poor students, but that the same requirements will also eliminate many who would be successful.[16]

The University of Kansas, in a more analytical study, has reported that about half of the freshmen admitted in 1951 were below the median on the national norms of the American Council on Education Psychological Examination. Of those who graduated from the university four years later, 800 were from the group above the median on the ACE, and 200 from the group below. Thus, if a "cutting score" for selective admission had been established at the median on the national norms, 200 of those who actually graduated would have been denied admission. If selection had been made at the same level but on the basis of a combination of scores on the aptitude test and an English placement test, 208 graduates would not have been admitted.[17] The loss would have been forty teachers, twenty-two engineers, five journalists, seven lawyers, seven doctors, seven pharmacists, and ninety-six graduates from the College of Liberal Arts and Sciences and the School of Business. In many of these fields manpower is short.

Many of these graduates participated in social and academic

[16] R. F. Berdie, "Some Principles and Problems of Selective College Admissions," *Journal of Higher Education,* vol. 31, pp. 191–199, April, 1960.

[17] The report states that "these same two tests (or tests just like them) make up at least half of the College Board Examination and a large part of all other batteries of selection tests used at the present time. They would be, as types, the first two to be chosen in any new set of examinations to be used to select incoming classes in state colleges or universities." But these institutions would be unlikely to select on the basis of these two test scores alone. They would undoubtedly include high school scholarship, preferably corrected for different standards among the schools.

organizations, and a substantial number attained positions of leadership. Of the 208 students, further, 29 were on a dean's scholastic honor roll during one semester, 2 during six semesters; 46 were on the honor rolls for at least one semester.

The percentage of graduating seniors who were below the 75th percentile on the ACE and English tests varied considerably from field to field. Of those who graduated from the School of Fine Arts, 73 per cent were below this level on the scholastic aptitude test, and 83 per cent below it on the English test. On the other hand, 48 per cent of the group in the College of Liberal Arts were below the 75th percentile on the aptitude test, and 68 per cent below it on the English test. About 44 per cent of the engineering group were below the top quartile on the aptitude test, and 80 per cent below it on the English examination. These data were used to point out that a minimum battery of rather general tests is almost certain to be extremely limited in differential prediction, that is, prediction of academic outcomes in various special fields.

The report also declared that every device for meeting mounting demands for admission should be tried before excluding students prior to enrollment.[18]

"THE RIGHT TO TRY" NEEDS
BROADER REFERENCE

Education for the ordinary man as well as for the talented, education for the humble occupations as well as for the learned callings—these have been the traditional purposes of the state university and the land-grant college. But it is not necessary for these institutions to remain equally comprehensive in the future.

Today it is appropriate to think of "the right to try" and of

[18] G. B. Smith, *Who Would Be Eliminated? A Study of Selective Admission to College*, Studies in Education, vol. 7, no. 1, University of Kansas, Lawrence, December, 1956.

preparation for a wide range of occupations as characteristics of American public higher education as a whole rather than as the responsibilities of the major state universities or of the major land-grant institutions.

TOWARD HIGHER STATUS

For the state universities, including the land-grant universities, to pitch their educational programs and standards at a higher level would not, as a matter of fact, play false with the course of their development. In their early days, the land-grant colleges required only an eighth grade certificate for admission, but this was ultimately raised to a high school diploma. As the preparation and quality of their students improved, these institutions made profound changes in the curriculum. A historian of the land-grant institutions has shown that they have moved far from the original intention of educating the industrial classes. The initial emphasis on agriculture and the mechanical arts has been broadened into the preoccupations of a modern university. The land-grant colleges, which began as trade schools, have won the struggle for status by elevating their specialized training to the level of professional education. Consequently, the colleges "are not preparing plumbers and mechanics, but engineers; not cooks and seamstresses but home economists; not so much practical farmers on the land as agricultural scientists." [19]

The change in agriculture and engineering from the practical to the professional paralleled the development of research to include both applied and fundamental investigation. Concerned first with practical problems, researchers found that these could not be solved without new advances in scientific knowledge. Hence they turned to the fundamental sciences. Previous work in organic chemistry led to the Babcock butterfat test; in bac-

[19] E. D. Eddy, *Colleges for Our Land and Time,* Harper & Brothers, New York, 1957, pp. 204, 280.

teriology, to successful control of plant and animal diseases; in theoretical genetics, to the development of hybrid corn; and in the sciences of growth and reproduction, to modern antibiotics.[20] All these basic sciences appear in the curricula of the land-grant colleges and universities, and instruction and research in these subjects are now recognized as fundamental to the development of the applied fields.

As agriculture and engineering became anchored more securely to the fundamental sciences, curricula made higher intellectual demands on students. It is true that especially colleges of agriculture still show a wide range of student ability and that some programs are more limited in their scientific demands than others; yet many graduate and undergraduate agricultural students compare favorably in intellectual capacity with the best in the basic sciences and the professions. Both in some land-grant institutions and in some of the other major state universities, the academic ability of entering students has been markedly improving. This change has been effected in most instances not so much by raising the formal requirements for admission as by counseling in high schools and at the universities themselves. Many students of limited ability, having learned the odds, decide not to lay their bets on success in the university. The widespread notion that there is little or no selection in the state universities is mistaken. The question is whether there should be more.

DIFFERENCES IN SELECTIVITY
OF STATE UNIVERSITIES

What is the ability level of entering students in the more selective state universities compared with that in less selective ones? The University of Minnesota, the University of Michigan at Ann Arbor, and the University of California at Berkeley may be taken as examples of greater selection.

[20] *Ibid.*, p. 282.

The University of Minnesota is a special case. Its doors are open to students with a wide range of ability, but two of its undergraduate divisions—the Institute of Technology and the College of Science, Literature, and the Arts—have a policy of selective admission of freshmen. A student may be admitted to the university but not to these divisions. Those excluded from the college and the institute may enter the two-year General College of the university.

The ability of the freshmen in the two more selective undergraduate divisions of the university may be seen against the background of differential selectivity among other four-year institutions in Minnesota. Approximately 68 per cent of the male freshmen of 1952 from Minnesota high schools who were enrolled in Minnesota colleges of all types came from the upper half of high school graduates in ability. The average ACE score of the entire group of Minnesota college freshmen was approximately the same as that in the Center's national sample, 104. The average ACE score of freshman men in the state colleges was 105, and of women, 103. The average score in seven non-Catholic, four-year liberal arts colleges was 112 for men and 115 for women.[21] The average score of the freshman men in the Institute of Technology of the University of Minnesota was 124, which represents a relatively high degree of selection over high school graduates; in the College of Science, Literature, and the Arts of the university, the score of the men was 122, and of the women, 119. The average high school percentile rank of men in the Institute of Technology was 74; of men in the College of Science, Literature, and the Arts, 69; and of women in the latter college, 82.

The average scholastic aptitude test score of the freshmen in the General College of the university, in contrast, was 90 for men and 85 for women; the average high school percentile ranks were

[21] The levels of ability in the groups of Minnesota colleges were not greatly different in 1958. Berdie et al., *op. cit.*

28 and 35. It is apparent that the University of Minnesota has enabled its four-year divisions to administer high standards of admission by creating a two-year college within the general university organization which less able students may enter.[22]

Of the freshmen in the several types of Minnesota institutions who came from the lower half of high school graduates, 40 per cent of the men and 32 per cent of the women in the state colleges were from the lower half in high school percentile rank, and 41 per cent and 39 per cent from that level in aptitude test scores. In the seven liberal arts colleges, the corresponding percentages were 23 and 13, and 30 and 22. In the Institute of Technology of the university, only 8 per cent of the men were from the lower half in high school percentile rank, and 10 per cent below the median in aptitude test scores. In the College of Science, Literature, and the Arts, the corresponding percentages were 12 and 10 for men, and 5 and 12 for women.

At the University of Michigan, the average ACE scores of the freshmen who entered in 1952, 1953, 1954, and 1955, equated to the 1952 form, varied from about 118 to 119 for the men and women together. By 1959, however, the average score had increased to 127, a substantial increase in selectivity. In the two colleges comparable to those for which University of Minnesota data were given, the averages in 1959 were approximately 125 and 127, somewhat higher than the Minnesota figures.[23]

The equivalent ACE mean score of the freshmen of 1956 in the College of Letters and Science of the University of California at Berkeley was 118, slightly lower than the mean scores of the freshman men and women of 1952 in the College of Science, Literature, and the Arts at the University of Minnesota, and

[22] Darley, *op. cit.*

[23] The data on test scores of the freshmen classes were supplied by the Bureau of Psychological Services, Evaluation and Examination Division, University of Michigan, Ann Arbor, and the equation to the 1952 form was made at the Center for the Study of Higher Education, University of California, Berkeley.

considerably lower than the mean of the freshmen of 1959 in the College of Letters, Science, and the Arts at the University of Michigan. At Berkeley, however, the mean score of freshmen in the Colleges of Agriculture, Architecture, and Chemistry, combined, was 129—much higher than in Letters and Science.[24]

The ability of freshmen in the Universities of Minnesota, Michigan, and California may be compared with that in two other state universities, one a separate land-grant institution with a large enrollment in arts and sciences and with numerous professional schools, and the other a single land-grant university.

In the first institution, the average freshman ACE score in 1959 was 108. (The average score of 1959 freshmen in 167 of the 200 institutions in the Center's 1952 national sample of higher institutions was about 109.) In the second institution, the ACE mean of 1952 freshmen was 111, although it is reported that there has been a slight general rise since that year, especially in the colleges of liberal arts and engineering, which were above the general mean of the freshmen in 1952.

MAJOR UNIVERSITIES SHOULD BECOME
STILL MORE SELECTIVE

It is clear that some state universities or, as in Minnesota, some of their divisions, have become fairly selective. It is entirely possible that they could become even more so and that they could limit their functions to those appropriate to an "institution of the highest grade" in the states in which a network of other public two-year and four-year institutions exists or in which such a network could be expanded or created. Other major state universities should move in the same direction. There is no intention to sug-

[24] Based on equivalent ACE scores computed by the Center for the Study of Higher Education from College Qualification Test Scores. "Test Scores of Berkeley, 'National' Freshmen," *University Bulletin*, vol. 6, no. 27, p. 117, University of California, 1958.

gest here how selective each of them should be or how rapidly each should raise its admission standards by formal or informal methods. Each will have to make the decision on the basis of plans for the future development of higher education in its own state.[25]

This is the general tenor of the proposals of the recent survey of higher education in Michigan. After commenting on the emergence of the University of Michigan as a highly selective institution heavily engaged in graduate and professional work, the report recommended that Michigan State University should also move toward greater selectivity and toward greater concentration on graduate education and research. It also proposed that junior colleges should be established in the Detroit metropolitan area to carry a large share of undergraduate enrollment and that Wayne State University should then inaugurate rigorous selection so as to concentrate on services comparable to those at the University of Michigan and Michigan State University.

The Michigan survey also recommended the strengthening of the other publicly supported four-year colleges and universities, which it conceived as regional institutions offering strong undergraduate work in the arts and sciences, education in such professional fields as business administration and engineering according to regional needs, and selected graduate programs. It proposed that certain institutions offer a two-year graduate curriculum in educational administration, the second year of which might be applied on the doctor's degree at one of the three major universities, and that this arrangement would be preferable for some years to the offering of the doctorate by all the institutions that

[25] A recent survey has shown that state-supported colleges and universities in only eleven states are required by law to accept any high school graduate in their own states "without regard to mental aptitude or other factors"; in thirty-nine states they are not required to do this, but in ten of these states the public institutions do so as a matter of policy. R. G. Lloyd, "Admission Policy in State-supported Higher Education," *School and Society*, vol. 88, pp. 446–447, Nov. 19, 1960.

prepare teachers and school administrators. Finally, the survey proposed that additional local community colleges be established according to a state-wide plan, with state assistance for both operating expense and capital outlay.

ADAPTATION TO PARTICULAR CONDITIONS

It has been said that a differentiated and coordinated system of public higher education is feasible only in states which have large, strong state universities. It is true that the possibility of moving rapidly toward such a system is greatest in such states as California, Michigan, Wisconsin, Illinois, and Ohio, which have strong major state universities and a network of state colleges or less highly developed public universities. A tripartite system like the one in California can be attained best where centers of population and financial resources will support strong community colleges. Many states are at a much earlier stage in the evolution of their universities and state colleges than those mentioned above, but with rapidly expanding enrollments and increasing pressure for new specialized educational services, these states, too, may face problems that have become acute where public higher education is well developed. They may be able to plan the future development of their public colleges and universities more rationally if they are aware of problems that have arisen elsewhere, often because of little or no research and coordinated planning. No state's system is completely exportable. Each state must work out a program that is consistent with its own traditions and its own cultural, economic, geographic, and demographic conditions. Iowa is not likely to adopt the California plan. It has only three four-year public institutions; most of its junior colleges are small, and there are few centers of population which would support large and diversified ones, although regional two-year institutions might be practicable. But there has been public controversy in the state recently over the roles and programs of the

University of Iowa, the Iowa State University (the land-grant institution), and the Iowa State Teachers College. Limited economic resources make sensible differentiation of functions and educational services among these three institutions mandatory. But with only one state college, which is not centrally located, and limited junior college enrollment, Iowa would find it difficult to adapt the California or Michigan system to its own needs. Its two universities will probably have to continue *through extensive internal differentiation* to serve the types of students and to provide the variety of educational services that could be more fully distributed *among* institutions in another state.

The division of responsibility and the relationships between public and private higher education is another factor to be considered in planning a state-supported system. College students in California are preponderantly in the public institutions. In New York, on the other hand, 60 per cent of the students are enrolled in private colleges and universities. The Heald Committee predicted, however, that this percentage will decline to something between 40 and 50 per cent (probably closer to the former) by 1985.[26] As public higher education in New York expands, not only will the relationships of the state-supported institutions to those privately controlled continue to be important, but the relationships of the former to one another *will be increasingly significant.*

The Heald Committee recommended that the eleven state teachers colleges (now called colleges of education) be converted into liberal arts colleges offering teacher education, that the community college system be expanded, that the state make additional provisions for nursing and medical education, and that graduate schools be established as integral parts of two new publicly supported universities.

[26] Committee on Higher Education (Henry T. Heald, Chairman), *Meeting the Increasing Demand for Higher Education in New York State,* State Education Department, Albany, 1960.

The master plan of the State University of New York went even further. It proposed not only that the colleges of education be transformed into liberal arts colleges but also that the colleges in Albany and Buffalo be developed immediately, and the others changed gradually into multipurpose institutions. The plan urged the creation of four, rather than two, graduate centers offering work for the doctorate.[27]

As this was being written, negotiations were under way for the State University to take over the University of Buffalo and develop it as one of its centers of graduate and professional education. During these negotiations the State University declared that it intended to maintain its College of Education at Buffalo and transform it, as proposed in the master plan, into a multipurpose institution.

Thus, in one city the State University would maintain a center for professional education and doctoral studies and a multipurpose college offering work through the master's degree, and would, in addition, be responsible for the supervision of the Erie County community college. In one metropolitan area the State University would immediately face the problems of differentiation and coordination, problems which it would meet as well in its state-wide organization.[28]

With the university centers and the state colleges under its immediate control, and with the community colleges under its general supervision, the State University will be in a position to organize, under its own aegis, a tripartite system of public higher education culminating in universities with selective admission and specialized functions.

[27] *The Master Plan,* State University of New York, Albany, 1961.
[28] The Regents of the University of the State of New York—which is not a university in the ordinary sense, but a policy-forming and administrative body—perform a broad coordinating function for both public and private higher education, since all institutions are "members" of the University of the State of New York. See Committee on Higher Education (Henry T. Heald, Chairman), *op. cit.*

There are likely to be stresses and strains in such a tripartite system, especially in coordinating institutions under more than one governing board—some of the tensions that occurred in California have already been illustrated—but the benefits to a state in making a distinguished university possible, in providing a wide range of educational opportunities, and in efficiently applying financial resources to educational needs far outweigh the difficulties of differentiating the functions and the services of the varied institutions in a system of public higher education.

THE DEVELOPMENT OF UNSTABLE
PARALLEL SYSTEMS

The effect of maintaining differential standards of admission and differential services is to establish parallel systems of higher education. Dr. Frank H. Bowles, president of the College Entrance Examination Board, has pointed out that the effect, in a single institution or system of colleges, of pushing standards so high that only the ablest students can meet them is "intellectual stratification and the formation of an elite." The alternative is to create a dual system, which, he maintains, already has been done. In one part of the system attrition is low, and more than half the students undertake graduate study in the dominant universities; this is the segment which trains for the learned professions, research, and the higher executive positions in business and government. In the other part of the system attrition is high, and few students go on to scholarly and higher professional careers. Most students from the institutions in this segment become technicians or specialists in a wide range of occupations for which high professional training is not required.

To the second segment, according to Bowles, belong most junior colleges and many four-year institutions, some of which have a large and complex organization. He believes that whereas the similarities have masked the differences between the two segments of the system, they will now break into separate systems, each with its own purposes and programs.[29]

In California two parallel systems—the university and the state colleges—are already well developed. But the differentiation between them is more unstable, and probably should be, than Bowles has indicated. Furthermore, the differences may not become as great as he implies. Reference has been made to the provision of the new *Master Plan for Higher Education in California* [30] for the conferring of doctoral degrees jointly by the university and the state colleges. This suggests that the state colleges, instead of becoming more unlike the university, will strive to meet university standards for the doctorate. It may take some time for any of the colleges to attain this in particular fields and a much longer time to achieve general university stature, but the road is open.

As a matter of fact, it would be unfortunate if the relationships between parallel systems of higher education became too rigid. As Riesman has observed, there have been notable instances of "social mobility," or, better, academic mobility, among colleges and universities. A sensible scheme of differential functions among higher institutions should not freeze their status, should not preclude the possibility of movement from one system to another. But it is essential for this to be a planned movement rather than a haphazard one.

It is conceivable that one or more of the California state colleges, or of the well-developed state colleges or secondary universities in other states, might move legitimately into the main university stream. But the difficulty of effecting this conversion should not be underestimated. Frequently, the faculty must be

---

[29] F. H. Bowles, "Patterns of Dominance and Choice," *Current Issues in Higher Education, 1959,* Association for Higher Education, Washington, 1959, p. 83.

[30] Master Plan Survey Team, *A Master Plan for Higher Education in California 1960–1975,* California State Department of Education, Sacramento, 1960.

reconstituted. Many of its original members, even if they have the scholarly background, are not likely to have the interests that characterize a university faculty with responsibility for advanced graduate study and research. Changing a college library into a university library is a colossal task entailing huge outlays. Supplying laboratory and research equipment and the buildings to house it is a costly operation. Only a few institutions provide the necessary foundation for remodeling, and no state can afford to reconstruct many, if they are to be universities of quality and distinction. Only a dramatic concentration and expansion of resources and support in a limited number of places will provide what is needed.

HAZARDS OF DECENTRALIZATION

It is proposed here to establish a relatively decentralized system of public higher education which gives the major university or universities primacy in research and in graduate and higher professional education, but not primacy in enrollment. One must admit, however, that there are hazards to the major universities in such a pattern. One of the hazards is that in making appropriations legislatures will pay more attention to the size of the enrollment than to the special purposes of the institution. Without question there is some budgetary danger in encouraging the great mass of freshmen and sophomores, many of whom will drop out by the end of the second year, to attend other institutions than the university. Many years ago a midwestern state university president, in urging the establishment of junior colleges, stated he was looking forward to the day when the university would become essentially an upper-division and graduate institution. Then the depression hit, and ultimately the university's enrollment declined. The president discovered that in a legislature that was short of funds, enrollment was the most potent factor in determining appropriations. Thereafter the state heard little from him about expanding the junior college system or about truncating the university.

There is some danger, too, in the fact that by curtailing its lower division the university will incur higher unit costs of instruction and other services. To put it crudely, a university "makes money" on its freshmen and sophomores, whom it ordinarily teaches mainly in large classes and often with teaching assistants or younger faculty members; and this surplus at the elementary level helps to support costly instruction at advanced undergraduate, professional, and graduate levels. Therefore, a university that wishes to become highly selective, that turns over a large share of its enrollment to junior colleges and state colleges for either terminal or preparatory training, must be ready to win support for a more expensive program—at least a program with higher unit costs.

A few examples will make the cost differential by level apparent. The California master plan has published up-to-date unit expenditures for the campuses of the University of California and the state colleges. Costs per student credit hour [31] were presented for teaching expense, departmental expense, and institutional expense.

Teaching expense was defined as the cost of salaries of instructors for the share of their time given to teaching plus the clerical salaries, supplies, and equipment related to instruction. The approximate teaching expense per student credit hour at the University of California at Los Angeles for the lower division was $11; for the upper division, $17; and for the graduate division, $67.

Institutional expense comprised all general and educational expenditures. The approximate unit costs at UCLA were $30, $45, and $181 for the three levels.[32]

[31] The number of student credit hours is the product of the credit-hour value of each course and the number of students enrolled in it. Thus thirty students in a three-credit-hour course would produce ninety student credit hours.

[32] Master Plan Survey Team, *op. cit.*, pp. 157–159.

It is apparent that over-all unit costs will be higher in an institution with a relatively small enrollment in the lower division and a primary emphasis on research and graduate education. Legislators and governmental budget officers are increasingly interested in unit costs, and an institution which will show high costs in comparison with others will have to be ready to justify greater expenditures in terms of differential functions and services.

CREATING A NEW IMAGE OF THE UNIVERSITY

Although a university that limits itself primarily to advanced instruction and research might face a difficult task in explaining to its legislature the reasons for higher unit costs, this is a task it should not shirk. In fact, it is a task which universities should have undertaken long since. The very fact that legislatures and executive departments tend to look at enrollments rather than functions is clear evidence that universities have been deficient in engendering public understanding of their mission. There are exceptions, of which the University of Michigan and the University of California are notable examples.

One of the first things this writer was told when he went to a principal state university nearly twenty-five years ago was never to reveal the hidden costs of research to the Legislature. The largest of these costs is the time used for research by faculty members whose salaries are charged entirely to instruction. With contracts and grants from many sources, a large part of the cost of research in the modern university is budgeted under, or charged to, "organized research." But a substantial expenditure is still represented by unallocated faculty research time.

Some state universities are still reluctant to reveal their total expenditures for research. The reluctance to make the cost of research a matter of record is shortsighted; it opens universities to unwarranted criticism for high unit costs of instruction. The fear that in a period of financial stringency legislatures will curtail appropriations for research if expenditures for this purpose are fully revealed is not irrational, of course. But the fear need not be so compelling if the university has made a continuing systematic effort to explain its essential functions and to create a public attitude favorable to their support. In the long run a university will gain more than it will lose if it makes a full accounting of its services.

This chapter closes, as it opened, with the contention that the major state universities should in fact become "institutions of learning of the highest grade." To that end, they should transfer their junior college functions to junior colleges; they should encourage the sound development of public, regional, four-year institutions offering instruction in liberal studies and selected professions; and they should concentrate their resources on advanced undergraduate, professional, and graduate education, on research, and on related levels of public service.

VII THE PEOPLE'S COLLEGE

American higher education has demonstrated a remarkable ability to expand during the past half century. The institution that has grown most rapidly is the junior college. By 1959, 22 per cent of the first-time and 12 per cent of the total enrollment in all higher institutions, and 19 per cent of the first-time and 11 per cent of the total enrollment in public institutions, was in the junior colleges.[1] The number and size of community colleges, technical institutes, or other types of two-year institutions should be increased further until they accommodate a still larger proportion of the youths who continue their education beyond the high school.

Before this proposition is discussed, a note on the history of the junior college movement is in point.

The junior college, an American innovation, apparently was born of an effort to reorganize the American university on the German model. The German student completed his general education and university preparation in the Gymnasium and at the

---

[1] *Opening Fall Enrollments in Higher Education, 1959, Analytic Report*, U.S. Department of Health, Education, and Welfare, Office of Education, 1960. Figures rounded.

age of nineteen or twenty entered the university to begin immediately upon his professional or specialized education.

Certain university presidents in the United States, familiar with the German system and impatient with the secondary school work that they declared composed most of the first two years of the four-year college of arts and sciences, proposed that the work of the freshman and sophomore years be relegated to the high schools. In the early 1850s President Henry P. Tappan of the University of Michigan, and in 1869 President William Watts Folwell of the University of Minnesota, urged such reorganization. About the turn of the century, at the University of Chicago, President William Rainey Harper entered the same plea. Although he believed that the first two years of the college should be transferred to two-year institutions or to upward extensions of the high schools, he took a compromise step at Chicago by dividing the undergraduate college horizontally into upper and lower divisions which he later called the junior college and the senior college. President David Starr Jordan of Stanford University recommended in 1907 that Stanford drop its freshman and sophomore years—a proposal that was not approved.

The proposals to eliminate the first two years of the four-year university college and to transform the American university into something like the German universities did not prevail. It is interesting that the final effort to make this transformation, or something like it, took place at the University of Chicago, where, influenced by Harper's ideas and by some administrators he found there when he became president, Robert M. Hutchins reorganized the university by snipping off the first two years and putting them into a new four-year college which included the last two years of the traditional high school. This plan of organization, however, was abandoned in 1953. The four-year liberal arts college proved to be a hardy institution.[2]

[2] J. S. Brubacher and W. Rudy, *Higher Education in Transition*, Harper & Brothers, New York, 1958, pp. 247–251. See also W. H.

Unable to eliminate its first two years, the University of Michigan had divided the undergraduate college into lower and upper divisions. Many other public universities, including the University of California, took the same step. An influential member of the University of California faculty, Alexis F. Lange, who became professor of education in 1906 and later dean of the school of education, aggressively promoted the establishment of junior colleges in California. He insisted that if the universities "are to thrive as universities," their work should rest on a foundation of fourteen years of elementary and secondary schooling. In 1917 he said that the university should retain the last two years of secondary education, but for a decreasing number of students, and that the university should absorb the last two years of the inherited four-year college to become something like the Continental university.[3]

Meanwhile, the California Legislature in 1907 had authorized the high schools to add two years of work beyond the standard four-year courses. The first community to take advantage of the enabling legislation was Fresno in 1910. The greatest growth of junior colleges in the state, however, dates from 1921, when the Legislature authorized the creation of special junior college districts.

Although the first public junior college was established elsewhere (at Joliet, Illinois), California was the state which embraced the junior college movement most enthusiastically; and in number of colleges, in enrollment, and perhaps in the fullest development of the community college idea, California has led the nation.

Cowley, "The War on the College," *Atlantic Monthly*, vol. 169, no. 6, June, 1942, pp. 719–726. Cowley declared that there had been eleven attempts to kill off the four-year college, all of which failed.

[3] Alexis F. Lange, "The Junior College as an Integral Part of the Public School System," *School Review*, vol. 25, no. 7, September, 1917, pp. 465–479.

CALIFORNIA JUNIOR COLLEGES
ASSUME A HEAVY LOAD

Although Stanford did not eliminate its lower division, David Starr Jordan remained a staunch advocate of the junior college. Through the years the University of California and Stanford have never faltered in their support. The junior college leaders of the state for many years had in President Robert Gordon Sproul of the University of California an enthusiastic proponent of the system. His successor, Clark Kerr, has also given it strong endorsement.

Although the effort to turn the first two years of the university over to the high school failed, it came closest to succeeding in California, where the University of California has encouraged students to take the first two years in the junior college and which has planned to reduce, but not to eliminate, the proportion of freshmen and sophomores in its undergraduate student body.

The *Restudy of the Needs of California in Higher Education* [4] recommended in 1955 that the University of California adopt the policy of reducing its lower-division enrollments in relation to those of the upper and graduate divisions and that the state colleges pursue a similar program. The Restudy report went on to list areas which were not well served by junior colleges and proposed that studies be made of the justification for establishing new ones in those communities. Later, following a study of the need for additional public higher institutions in California, the Regents of the University and the State Board of Education endorsed the principle that adequate junior college facilities should be provided through local initiative and state assistance before the establishment of additional state college or university cam-

[4] T. C. Holy, T. R. McConnell, and H. H. Semans, *A Restudy of the Needs of California in Higher Education,* California State Department of Education, Sacramento, 1955, p. 44.

puses.[5] (The State Legislature failed to follow this principle in establishing one state college, which, however, opened as an upper-division institution, with the understanding that the introduction of a lower division would wait upon the organization of a junior college in the community.)

The new California master plan of 1960 went even further than the Restudy in proposing to divert future enrollment from the state colleges and the university campuses to the public junior colleges. It recommended that 50,000 students who would otherwise enter the state colleges and the university in 1975 should be shunted to public junior colleges. To that end, the plan proposed that the proportion of undergraduates in the lower divisions of all public four-year institutions be gradually reduced by 10 percentage points below the percentage in 1960. This would bring the university's lower-division enrollment to about 37 per cent of the undergraduate total, or 24 per cent of the entire student body, undergraduate and graduate.[6]

The master plan reaffirmed the principle that no new state colleges or campuses of the university, other than those already approved, be established until adequate junior college facilites had been provided and recommended that the new state college and university campuses previously approved by the Legislature be limited to upper-division and graduate work until adequate junior college opportunities had been provided in the primary areas served by these institutions. The plan offered evidence of the need for establishing twenty-two more junior colleges. The plan also recommended that between 1960 and 1975 the state gradually increase the operating support for the junior colleges

    [5] H. H. Semans and T. C. Holy, *A Study of the Need for Additional Centers of Public Higher Education in California*, California State Department of Education, Sacramento, 1957, pp. iii-vi.
    [6] Master Plan Survey Team, *A Master Plan for Higher Education in California 1960–1975*, California State Department of Education, Sacramento, 1960, pp. 59, 62.

from 30 per cent to 45 per cent and that the state aid local communities in making capital outlays for junior colleges.

SUCCESS OF JUNIOR COLLEGE
TRANSFER STUDENTS

These sweeping proposals are based on a sound record of accomplishment by the junior colleges in preparing students for successful upper-division work in the state's four-year colleges and universities. For example, on the Berkeley campus of the University of California, junior college transfer students who would have been eligible for admission to the university at the time of high school graduation perform about as well as "native" students in grade-point average and persistence. Students who would have been ineligible for admission at the time of high school graduation, but who became eligible by attending a junior college, are less successful than native students. On the Los Angeles campus of the university, however, the record of students who entered as freshmen is somewhat better than that of the "eligible" junior college transfers.

In his national survey of junior colleges, conducted under the auspices of the Center for the Study of Higher Education, Medsker made a study of the academic records of junior college transfers in sixteen institutions (all but one of which were public colleges or universities) in nine states. He concluded that in general the transfer students did somewhat less well then the native students in the first term after transfer but that in most institutions by the end of the senior year they closely approached, and in a few instances did slightly better than, the native students. The differentials tended to be not more than three-tenths of a grade point and were often less. In persistence, however, the transfers were inferior: in most institutions, their retention rate during the junior and senior years was markedly lower than that of the native students. Medsker also reported that a larger percentage of transfer students took longer than the normal time to complete the requirements for the degree.[7]

In only one of the institutions included in the study were the transfer and native students matched for ability. In this instance, the transfer students were more successful in grades and persistence. This was also true in a study made previously at Washington State College.[8] A study at the University of Colorado, however, was somewhat inconclusive. In the first semester of the senior year, the grade-point average of the native students was slightly higher in the College of Arts and Science and in the School of Business, but slightly lower in the College of Engineering.[9]

The reasons for the poorer persistence of transfer students are not clear. Individual institutions in the Medsker study reported that attrition was by no means always due to poor scholarship. Unidentified selective factors other than intelligence probably played a significant role. The fact that many junior college students come from lower socioeconomic groups suggests that both financial and motivational factors may contribute to poor persistence. Failure of the four-year institution to orient transfer students to a new academic environment, which often makes higher and different intellectual demands, may also place them at a disadvantage with experienced students. But the possibility of less effective preparation in the junior college cannot be ruled out until more careful studies of the causes of withdrawal are made.

[7] L. L. Medsker, *The Junior College: Progress and Prospect,* McGraw-Hill Book Company, Inc., New York, 1960, pp. 131–135.

[8] S. V. Martorana and L. L. Williams, "Academic Success of Junior College Transfers at the State College of Washington," *Junior College Journal,* vol. 24, pp. 402–415, March, 1954.

[9] A. W. Hall, "The Academic Success of Junior College Transfers to the Junior Level at the University of Colorado," unpublished doctoral dissertation, University of Colorado, Boulder, 1958.

An intensive study in ten states of the academic success of transfer students in comparison with native students is now being conducted at the Center under Medsker's direction. Investigation was undertaken at the instance of the Committee on Junior and Senior Colleges composed of representatives of the American Association of Collegiate Registrars and Admissions Officers, the American Association of Junior Colleges, and the Association of American Colleges. Among the subjects being investigated are the causes of withdrawal, the characteristics of students who drop out, and the extent to which the apparent satisfactory performance of transfer students is due to the withdrawal of those who make poor academic records.

Pending the outcome of this study, it seems reasonable to conclude that a properly developed junior college system can provide satisfactory preparatory training for students who transfer to four-year institutions, leaving the major universities free to concentrate on advanced curricula, provided there is close coordination between the two- and four-year institutions, with continuing efforts to clarify for the junior colleges the nature of, and prerequisites for, advanced undergraduate education of high quality.

The system of "articulation committees" in California is a good example of effective cooperation. A joint committee of the University of California and the public junior colleges meets semiannually for two consecutive days with a carefully prepared agenda, and other joint committees discuss content and instructional procedures in junior college courses which will be offered for transfer credit at the university. There also are articulation committees on preprofessional curricula in architecture and engineering. The University of California must approve all courses which will be submitted for advanced standing from the junior colleges. Thus, the California junior colleges develop their transfer programs with the continuing guidance of the university. Furthermore, the university sends periodic reports of the academic performance of transfer students to the junior colleges from which they came as a means of aiding the latter to evaluate their preparatory work.

MISGIVINGS ABOUT EXCEPTIONAL STUDENTS

The summary given above of the success of transfer students was based on group statistics and reveals nothing about the performance of either the most or the least able students. Misgivings have been expressed about the value of junior college attendance for gifted students. Riesman recently observed that it is difficult to see how attending a junior college represents a real break for a student who may have classes in a high school building, under some of the same teachers or at least teachers of the same type as he had in high school, and in courses not greatly different from those he had before. The implication is that going to college should represent a psychological leap from home, old associates, and old ways of learning and thinking, to a new, invigorating, intellectual environment with expectations of social and emotional, as well as intellectual, maturity and independence in what Riesman called "a more astringent setting."

Riesman believes that students should be forced to decide whether they should go to college, even if it entails personal sacrifices for them and their families, rather than being allowed "to drift on as shoppers or passive customers, half in and half out, half at college and half at home, dropping in and dropping out." He would prefer a strong program of adult education rather than "a dilution of the concept of college to meet a sliding scale of eagerness." [10]

Riesman's picture of junior college students meeting in high school classrooms and taking courses very much like those they had studied in high school is hardly an up-to-date snapshot. Many

[10] David Riesman, "College Subcultures and College Outcomes," in T. R. McConnell (ed.), *Selection and Educational Differentiation*, Field Service Center and Center for the Study of Higher Education, University of California, Berkeley, 1960, pp. 1–14.

junior colleges, not only in California but in other states as well, have handsome, separate campuses, and they make special efforts to model their courses on lower-division university courses; they are often even too eager to use the same textbooks and syllabuses.

It is worth remembering, too, that junior colleges are not the only institutions with large numbers of local students. The state universities and some of the private universities in urban centers also have many commuting students. These students, too, are "half in and half out, half at college and half at home." While for these students the break between high school and university may be greater than that between high school and local junior college, the psychological jump is smaller than for students who leave home to go to school. Yet their presence in a college community with a substantial segment of resident students and with its complex of specialized departments and professional schools should create for local students some sense of a new and decisive beginning, the awareness of membership in a more cosmopolitan society. We may hope so, for the urban college or university, with its great body of commuters, will enroll a large percentage of college students in the years to come.

Yet Riesman's concern about the student who merely drifts from high school to junior college cannot be wished away. In entering the junior college, students may lack the sense of having made a decisive transition, largely because the college itself has often failed to attain a clear identity. One reason for the difficulty in developing a distinctive image is that the junior college has an ambiguous status in the American educational system. Legally, it is usually defined as a part of secondary education, and with elementary schools and high schools it may be part of a unified school system and a unified school district. Yet it is increasingly considered to be allied with higher education. This ambiguity handicaps the junior college in attaining a clear-cut identity, status, and role, and, in turn, blurs for the student the transition from school to college.

These problems have been highlighted in a case study of the

development of the San Jose City College in California. This junior college is admittedly atypical in California, but it may be used to raise sharply the problems of identity and student image of the institution. The general level of student ability and achievement in the college was low. The median scholastic aptitude score of the student body was well below the national median for college students. It was a "working class" junior college. Fewer than a fourth of its students from San Jose were from business and professional families, while two-thirds of them had fathers in "blue collar" occupations. Many students who were in fact "terminal," that is, who did not transfer to senior colleges, were nevertheless enrolled in transfer courses. These were called "latent terminals." Their presence in transfer courses created instructional problems for teachers who had to prepare more able and more highly motivated students for senior college work.

Administratively the junior college was a part of a unified school district rather than the creature of a separate junior college district with an autonomous governing board. This tended to tie the college to the educational policies, the personnel practices, and, to a considerable degree, the image of the public school system. The administrative staff members were selected from within the district and had "assimilated its philosophy and learned to accept its authority." Their background was predominantly in elementary and secondary education.

Two out of three full-time teachers had been drawn from high school positions; few had had experience in four-year colleges. Their teaching loads were heavy, more like those characteristic of high schools than of colleges. They were on the same salary schedule as the high school teachers and they did not enjoy professorial titles or ranks. Fewer than 5 per cent had a doctor's degree.

In various ways the staff members who had had only public school experience adhered more closely to educational policies and attitudes characteristic of public secondary education than did those who had had experience in four-year institutions. The latter were more likely than the former to consider scholastic requirements for admission too low, to agree that the junior college was too much like a glorified high school, to believe that the students were frequently overcounseled, and to say there was too much stress on size of enrollment and too little on educational quality. Those with high school background, on the other hand, were more likely to agree that an important function of the junior college is to relieve the four-year institutions of the burden of undergraduates not academically inclined and that four-year colleges have too much influence on junior college curricula.[11]

The degree of organizational and administrative autonomy is another factor determining status and identity. The San Jose City College is administratively dependent on the larger unified school system, a relationship which sharply limits its freedom to choose its students, to establish its educational policy, to select its administrative and instructional personnel, and to determine its curriculum. Its self-image, as well as the community's perception of its status, would be enhanced if it were controlled and financed by a separate junior college district. In a study of the attitudes of junior college administrators and instructors in unified districts, two-thirds of both groups declared that a junior college should be autonomous.[12]

Although an analysis of organizational forces seems, on balance, to be in favor of the autonomous junior college district, some junior colleges in unified districts are apparently as effective and distinctive as those administratively independent. The former evidently have surmounted the handicaps of dependency by attaining a high degree of self-determination, physical separation, and an atmosphere that marks them as colleges rather than extensions of the high school.

[11] B. R. Clark, *The Open Door College: A Case Study*, McGraw-Hill Book Company, Inc., New York, 1960.
[12] Medsker, *op. cit.*, p. 313.

The ambiguity of the role of the unselective junior college is inherent in its service as a comprehensive community institution. In a hierarchical system of higher education, it protects every student's "right to try." In spite of its heterogeneous population, it is judged by one segment of its community, by many of its own faculty, and by the academic world in general by its ability to prepare students for successful work in four-year institutions. Another part of the community evaluates it by its effectiveness in supplying technicians for local industries, businesses, and professions. It is in effect a great distributive center, selecting *after admission* the students capable of succeeding in four-year colleges and giving them an academic regimen, while at the same time coping with the "latent terminals" and encouraging as many of them as might profit from it to shift to an occupational curriculum.[13] All this the junior college must do without making the screening function too obvious. Nevertheless, despite its many-sided character, it should be able to attain a better identity and a clearer status by articulating its multiple responsibilities for itself, its students, and its community.

For the transfer student, the junior college may create a sense of having taken a step in personal development by making him responsible for his own learning, by encouraging intellectual independence, and by challenging him to the full use of his capacities. This task requires a faculty with serious intellectual interests and scholarly attitudes, even if it is expected to be tolerant of other functions of the junior college than the preparation of students for advanced undergraduate study.

By these and other means, the junior colleges may be able, in some part at least, to meet Riesman's reservations concerning their collegiate function. These institutions are attended by many capable students who would be unable to go to college if it meant

[13] The term "latent terminal" was used by Clark to refer to those who may be identified or self-classified as transfer students but who do not transfer.

leaving home; spending two years locally may make four years possible for students who would otherwise have been unable to finance a full undergraduate course. Nevertheless, in the writer's judgment, the ablest students should have an opportunity to attend a selective college or university rather than a local unselective institution, whether of two- or four-year status. To this end, scholarships and stipends should be available when necessary to the largest possible number of such students. Since many of the ablest students need the stimulus of a cosmopolitan and intellectually demanding environment and the opportunity for advanced courses, individual study, and research, the selective university should not abandon its lower division entirely.

THE EXPANDING JUNIOR COLLEGE MOVEMENT

On balance, the record and the potentialities considered, the current and imminent expansion of the junior college movement is well justified. This writer agrees with Dr. Conant's statement, quoted earlier, that "there should be no inconsistency with our educational ideals if local two-year colleges were to enroll as many as half of the boys and girls who wished to engage in formal studies beyond the high school."

California is not the only state proceeding in this direction. The Illinois Commission of Higher Education has recommended that no new branches of public institutions be established in the state until designated communities have had an opportunity to make thorough studies of the need to establish community two-year colleges,[14] and it has recommended that new community colleges be established in thirteen locations.[15] Likewise, the final report of a survey of higher education in Michigan opposed the

[14] Illinois Commission of Higher Education, *Annual Report, 1958,* Chicago, 1959.

[15] Illinois Commission of Higher Education, *Annual Report, 1960,* Chicago, 1961.

establishment of additional branches of existing state educational institutions and recommended, instead, a considerable expansion of the community college system, not so much as a means of draining future enrollments from the existing four-year public institutions, as for the purpose of extending and equalizing educational opportunity for the youths of the state.[16]

The Heald Committee on Higher Education in New York,[17] the regents' proposals for the expansion of higher education in New York,[18] Governor Nelson A. Rockefeller's special message to the Legislature on the state's needs in higher education,[19] and the master plan of the State University of New York [20] all have recommended the establishment of more community colleges. "Experience with the community college program indicates," said Governor Rockefeller, "that the two-year community colleges— low tuition, State-aided, locally-supported and administered— will provide an essential and major part of the higher educational opportunities in New York State in the years ahead."

Many other states, some of which have had few or no public community colleges, are proposing to establish two-year institutions or to add additional ones.

Florida launched what is probably the most carefully prepared program for the development of public junior colleges. In 1955 the State Legislature established the Community College Council

[16] J. D. Russell, *The Final Report of the Survey of Higher Education in Michigan,* Michigan Legislative Study Committee on Higher Education, Lansing, September, 1958.

[17] Committee on Higher Education (Henry T. Heald, Chairman), *Meeting the Increasing Demand for Higher Education in New York State,* State Education Department, Albany, 1960.

[18] *The Regents' Proposals for the Expansion and Improvement of Education in New York State, 1961,* State Education Department, Albany, 1960.

[19] N. A. Rockefeller, *Expanded Opportunities and Facilities for Higher Education,* State of New York, Legislative Document no. 9, 1961.

[20] *The Master Plan,* State University of New York, Albany, 1961.

and directed it to formulate a long-range plan for the establishment and coordination of community colleges. In its report to the
State Board of Education, the council stated that if the barriers
to continued education were to be eliminated, Florida would require the eventual establishment of twenty-seven new junior
college areas. It estimated that thirty-one areas would enable 99
per cent of the state's young people to attend a college within approximately thirty miles of their homes. The council promulgated
basic policies to guide the development of the junior colleges; outlined a procedure for development of the state-wide plan; defined
criteria for determining the areas where the institutions were
needed; asked representatives of local communities to make surveys of needs, resources, interest, and probable support in their
areas; and, on the basis of all these considerations, set up priorities
for the creation of the new two-year colleges.[21]

Florida is making rapid progress in carrying out its program.
Four new community colleges were opened in 1960, and four
more have been recommended for consideration by the Legislature in 1961, which would bring the total to eighteen. In 1960
the fourteen junior colleges then operating in the state enrolled
68,000 students, amounting to 23 per cent of all college students
and 43 per cent of all college freshmen in the state.

RESISTANCE TO JUNIOR COLLEGES IN OHIO

The problem in Ohio is different from that in the states discussed so far. Ohio has no public junior colleges. Many proponents
of public community colleges in the state have had the impression
that the four-year institutions, public and private, have been reluctant to see junior colleges established in spite of the fact that in
a survey conducted under the auspices of the Ohio College Asso-

[21] Community College Council, *The Community Junior College in
Florida's Future*, Florida State Department of Education, Tallahassee,
1957.

ciation, Dr. John Dale Russell, drawing on many studies made over the years at the Ohio State University,[22] pointed out great differences in the percentage of young people going to college in counties which had colleges or universities within their boundaries and in counties which did not have them. A high school graduate in a county with a state or municipal university had two and one-half or three times the chance of going to college as one in a county without a college. In 1954–1955 the proportion of college-age youths in college was less than 20 per cent in sixty-eight out of eighty-four counties and less than 10 per cent in sixteen counties.[23] In 1959–1960 still no more than 23 per cent of college-age youths were in full-time attendance in the state at large.[24] The survey director concurred with the "large majority" of those he interviewed in the judgment that educational opportunity should be expanded by establishing publicly supported community colleges offering both transfer and terminal curricula, with heavy emphasis on the latter.[25] He conceded that an early start on this program might be made by setting up branches of existing state universities but insisted that such branches should be transformed into separate institutions of the "true community college type" as soon as possible.

After the Russell survey, on the recommendation of the Ohio College Association, the governor appointed a Commission on Education beyond High School, which proposed that existing colleges and universities should establish branches justified by local need and support but also recommended that the General Assembly should enact permissive legislation for the creation of

[22] D. H. Eikenberry, *The Need for Upward Extension of Secondary Education in Ohio*, Ohio State University, College of Education, Columbus, 1954.
[23] J. D. Russell, *Meeting Ohio's Needs in Higher Education*, Ohio College Association, Wooster, 1956, pp. 29–33.
[24] I am indebted to President J. D. Millett of Miami University for this information.
[25] Russell, *op. cit.*, p. 116.

two-year colleges or technical institutes supported by state appropriations, local funds, and tuition. The commission proposed that the same form of support should be given to the branches of four-year institutions.

With the support of the Ohio School Boards Association and the Ohio Education Association, a bill was introduced in 1959 in the Ohio General Assembly authorizing local school districts to establish institutions offering two-year programs of technical education beyond the high school and enough transfer work to permit qualified students to proceed to four-year colleges. These institutions were to be locally governed, but the state would provide up to one-half their capital costs and one-third their operating expenditures.

The Ohio College Association favored the postponement of this legislation until a more carefully devised program for the development of two-year colleges could be prepared. Nevertheless, the Assembly passed the bill, only to have it vetoed by the governor because (among other reasons) no funds had been appropriated to carry out the act's provisions.

On the recommendation of the Commission on Education beyond High School, the Assembly authorized the creation of an Interim Commission on Education beyond the High School composed of nine members appointed by the governor. Reporting in 1961, this commission recommended legislation that would authorize a county or combination of counties having a population of at least 100,000 to establish a junior college district to be governed by a board of trustees consisting of seven local members appointed by the governor for overlapping five-year terms. The board would be empowered to decide whether the junior college should be operated entirely by the district itself or whether the college should be operated wholly or in part under contract with an accredited university or college. The proposed legislation would create a state community college board to give supervision and leadership to the local junior colleges. This board would be composed of the governor or his representative and six members appointed by the governor, with the advice and consent of the Senate, for overlapping six-year terms. The state superintendent of public instruction and one president of an accredited four-year college would serve as advisory members of the board at the pleasure of the governor.

The local community college board would be empowered to borrow funds for the construction of the plant, the debt service to be carried by a general property tax in the local community college district. The operating income would be obtained from student fees and appropriations by the Legislature.

The college would be allowed to conduct transfer courses for college credit, technical and subprofessional curricula, and college level adult education courses.[26]

In the meantime, the six state universities have established twenty-nine local two-year branches in various urban communities. In October, 1960, more than 10,000 students were enrolled in the branches then in existence. The overwhelming proportion of this enrollment was part time, varying from about 25 per cent to 90 per cent among the branches.[27] In the fall semester, 1958, about 1,200 full-time students had enrolled in the twenty-two branches then in existence.[28] Between 1950 and 1960 the part-time enrollment in the state universities increased 225 per cent.[27] At present, the branches confine their offerings for the most part to evenings and Saturdays in the classrooms of the local high school.

There is vigorous debate between the proponents of university branches and the advocates of community colleges. The former point out that branches would not face the problem of accredita-

[26] *A Proposed Policy for the State of Ohio for Community Colleges and University Branches*, Ohio Interim Commission on Education beyond the High School, Columbus, 1961. (Mimeographed.)

[27] Data supplied by Dr. J. D. Millett.

[28] Medsker, *op. cit.*, p. 261.

tion, as would new local two-year institutions; that the present branches are located in most of the centers of population, and when a full-time enrollment of 500 students is attained, permanent day-time facilities can be provided; and that technical education based on community needs could be offered by the branches.[29]

What the presidents of the state universities most fear about the movement to establish community colleges is the further diffusion of the state's financial support of higher education. This concern has been expressed as follows: "If independent junior or community colleges are started, they will have to be almost wholly subsidized. The tax dollars that can be made available will then be spread thin. The existing state universities will suffer; the new institutions will have to be held to minimum levels, and mediocrity may be shared by all." [30]

The case for community colleges has been summarized in an editorial in the *Educational Research Bulletin* of Ohio State University: [31]

> Community colleges have developed in large numbers over the country and have proved their worth. They can respond to local needs with a facility that branches controlled from a distance by large and complex institutions would have great difficulty in doing. Their development has enhanced interest in education and helped bring about increased support for it. Moreover, as many students of higher education have pointed out, our senior institutions can render their greatest service in the years ahead by giving increased attention to advanced liberal-arts, professional, and graduate instruction, and to research. Responsibility for all

[29] F. J. Tate, "The Case for Expanding Branch Campuses," *Ohio State University Monthly*, pp. 5–7, January, 1961.
[30] *Ibid.*
[31] *Educational Research Bulletin*, vol. 40, pp. 48–49, College of Education, Ohio State University, Feb. 8, 1961.

state-supported education beyond the high school would hamper rather than further this proper work.

The interest of leaders in the public school system of the state—and possibly a lessening of opposition by the four-year institutions—will probably lend impetus to the development of local two-year colleges in Ohio. But what general pattern will evolve from the advantages claimed for university branches, technical institutes, and comprehensive community colleges is not yet clear.

OPPOSITION IN INDIANA

In Indiana the establishment of local two-year colleges has been openly opposed. President H. B. Wells of Indiana University has contended that the present institutional framework in most states, especially those east of the Rocky Mountains, can be expanded sufficiently to accommodate the rush of additional students. He pointed out that educational institutions are so well distributed in Indiana that 92 per cent of all high school graduates can at least begin their college work within twenty-five miles of their homes.

Wells warned especially against the development of a public junior college system: [32]

> The establishment of large numbers of additional colleges would represent an unnecessary dilution of taxpayer financial support and a heavy drain on the resources of private and church groups. A *special* word of caution is in order with respect to the establishment of junior or community colleges in those states which already have a large number of four-year institutions.

Indiana and Purdue universities have pursued the policy of establishing local extension centers, which are the only two-year

[32] H. B. Wells, "The Outlook for Higher Education in America," *Proceedings of the Eleventh Annual National Conference on Higher Education,* Association for Higher Education, Washington, 1956, pp. 1–9.

public colleges in the state. Indiana University maintains nine branches, and Purdue four. Both institutions operate centers in Fort Wayne and Indianapolis. In the first semester of 1958–1959, the Indiana University branches enrolled 1,214 full-time students, 8,000 part-time students in courses giving university credit, and more than 5,200 part-time students in noncredit courses. The university offers mainly standard lower-division courses in the liberal arts and in business. As of spring, 1960, it had established no terminal curricula but planned to do so, particularly in business. Purdue, on the other hand, offers two-year programs for engineering technicians in all four of its centers. In the fall of 1958 these centers enrolled more than 2,200 students in lower-division, degree-credit courses and more than 2,300 in technical institute curricula; these figures include full- and part-time students.[33]

EXTENSION CENTERS VERSUS JUNIOR COLLEGES

Pennsylvania and Wisconsin also have followed the pattern of off-campus extension centers or branches. (Pennsylvania has one public junior college, and pressure for more is growing.) It is apparent that not all universities are ready to accept Conant's proposal to be content not to grow in enrollment but to aim at a different distribution of aptitudes and interests in their undergraduate student bodies. Conant said:[34]

> For those who regard universities as first of all institutions for research, scholarly work, and professional education, the advantages in changing the composition of the entering class are obvious. That is to say, there is not need to argue the case to those who understand the significance of having the lead-

[33] Medsker, *op. cit.*, pp. 227–230.
[34] J. B. Conant, *The Citadel of Learning*, Yale University Press, New Haven, Conn., 1956, pp. 70–73.

ers of the free world educated professionally on campuses where the scholarly spirit of free inquiry is dominant.

But if the point is obvious, university presidents who have established or are hastening to set up branches or extension centers do not act accordingly. This device presumably holds down the enrollment on the central campus, but it probably does not change the intellectual composition of the undergraduate student body. With the vast prospective increase in college enrollment, one might have expected the large state colleges and universities willingly to abandon their roles as great junior colleges. But such does not seem to be their policy. These institutions still wish to keep the great mass of students in their own folds; they evidently are unwilling to share the tax dollar even with community colleges, although their support is likely to come only in part from state funds. Whatever the advantages in monopolizing the state's financial contribution to higher education, one might ask whether the university branches are likely to serve the people's needs as fully as would two-year, locally controlled community colleges.

In his study of two-year colleges Medsker visited university branches in several states and interviewed the officials on the central campuses who were administratively responsible for the outlying institutions. In appraising the relative merits of branches versus community colleges, he came to the following conclusions:

1. The curriculum in most extension centers is much less diversified than in community colleges. With a limited number of exceptions, the extension centers included in the study offered only transfer curricula.

2. In a zealous and commendable effort to make academic standards in the branches comparable to those on the main campus, the supervision of the central university left little opportunity for the extension centers to develop personalities of their

own. Studies of the performance of transfer students have shown that university control is not necessary to assure the success of junior college graduates in four-year institutions.

3. The tendency for the parent university to make the centers either wholly or partially self-supporting—and sometimes to generate the funds for capital outlay—often at the expense of charging much higher fees than those assessed on the main campus, fosters financial instability and, frequently, inadequate budgets and facilities.

4. The higher tuition charges in extension centers than in public junior colleges in other states suggests that young people from low-income families may be better able to continue their education when junior colleges are available.

In a recent study of college-going in communities in which different kinds of public institutions are located—junior colleges, four-year state colleges, extension centers, or combinations of these types—Medsker found that the communities in which the highest percentage of local high school graduates entered college were those which had junior colleges. He found, also, that communities with extension centers and those with no colleges were almost equal in the percentage of high school graduates who continued their education. The junior colleges did not attract merely local students of mediocre ability; in the communities in which they were located, a higher percentage of high-ability students entered college than in communities with other kinds of institutions.

Medsker conceded that neither the advantages nor the disadvantages were all on the side of branches or community colleges and that particular conditions would determine which would be preferable in given states, but he strongly advocated a comprehensive two-year institution geared broadly to local or regional needs. He declared that for a state university to engage in state-wide or regional expansion through a system of branches or extension centers "as a means of eliminating a system of two-year colleges which would be a potential competitor" would not be in the best interests of the state and its youths.[35]

In his study of the coordination of public higher education, Glenny pointed out that a system of two-year university branches may impede diversity in types of institutions, educational programs, or modes of control. He observed, also, that the branch pattern tends to impose not only standardization but also centralization on a state's system of higher education. The very university administrators who most strenuously oppose formal coordination on the ground that it is conducive to standardization are often the ones who have established two-year branches which lead to the same end so far as lower-division instruction is concerned.[36]

Although the community college may be expected to relieve four-year institutions of the main burden of elementary instruction, this is by no means its only, or even its principal, justification. It performs other functions which are worthy in their own right. It enables many capable students to attend college who would otherwise find it financially impossible to do so. It opens its doors to students of more limited ability who nevertheless may deserve some formal training beyond the twelfth grade, if not a four-year course. In these two senses it widens opportunity; it assures the "right to try" in a system of higher education with a progressive increase in selectivity from two-year institutions to regional state colleges to centralized universities. The community college sorts out the students who have a good chance of doing successful work in four-year institutions and offers alternatives for those who are either uninterested in advanced education or

[35] Medsker, *op. cit.*, pp. 308–312.
[36] L. A. Glenny, *Autonomy of Public Colleges: The Challenge of Coordination*, McGraw-Hill Book Company, Inc., New York, 1959, pp. 218–266.

deficient in ability. It provides for the terminal student the first level of the training in general and technical education which is the requisite of a democratic, industrialized social order. "An important effect of the unselective college," said Clark, "is to permit a system of higher education as a whole to be both 'democratic' and 'selective.' " [37]

[37] Clark, *op. cit.*, p. 167. Reference has been made to the fact that although two-thirds of the students in junior colleges are in transfer curricula, only one-third actually transfer to four-year institutions. One of the important functions of the junior college, in Clark's view, is that of inducing the "latent terminal" of limited ability to acquire a more realistic conception of his aptitudes and to change his aspirations. The junior college, unlike the typical university with its high attrition during the first and second years, offers the student a choice of alternatives, enabling him to save face personally and socially and to embark on a constructive terminal educational program or to enter the world of work.

VIII THE CONSTRUCTIVE ROLE
OF COORDINATION

The tendency of institutions to strive for similarity rather than distinctiveness has already been emphasized. Some of the impediments to purposeful variation have also been noted. But however real and persistent the problems of institutional differentiation, the consequences of unnecessary duplication are often unfortunate: (1) failure to provide the types and levels of education which would most fully capitalize our varied human resources and most adequately meet our diverse civic, cultural, and industrial needs; and (2) inefficient and uneconomical utilization of the financial resources available for higher education. The former deficiency is the more serious. The latter problem becomes acute when quality is at stake and when highly specialized and advanced levels of education are concerned.

EXPANSION OF COORDINATION

The increasing complexity of higher education, limited financial resources, and competition among public institutions for

136

available funds early led some of the less wealthy states to establish some type of formal coordination.

The formal coordinating agencies are of two general types: (1) a single board which coordinates and governs either all public higher institutions in a state, such as the Oregon State Board of Education, or all institutions of a particular system within a state, such as the Trustees of the State College System, which controls the state colleges; and (2) an overriding board, sometimes called a "superboard," empowered to coordinate and to control selected activities of institutions or systems of institutions without displacing their own boards of trustees. An example is the Board of Educational Finance in New Mexico.[1] Voluntary coordinating bodies, of which the Ohio Inter-University Council is an example, also have been established in several states.

Although most coordinating agencies were first established in economically limited states, the problem of coordination is no longer confined to them. With burgeoning enrollments and mounting demands on state funds, some of the wealthier states have now created formal or voluntary coordinating bodies, and others are likely to follow. We have already mentioned the creation of the Illinois Commission of Higher Education, which was given a mandate to recommend a plan for "the unified administration of all the State-controlled institutions of higher education"; the commission did not recommend a plan for the unified administration of these institutions but did propose to the Legislature a Board of Higher Education to coordinate them. Formal

[1] One of the first projects of the Center for the Study of Higher Education in its studies of educational diversity was a description and evaluation of methods of state-wide coordination of public colleges and universities. The results of this investigation are published in L. A Glenny, *Autonomy of Public Colleges: The Challenge of Coordination*, McGraw-Hill Book Company, Inc., New York, 1959. This volume includes analyses of the organization and operation of all major types of coordinating agencies. See also S. V. Martorana and Ernest V. Hollis, *State Boards Responsible for Higher Education*, U.S. Department of Health, Education, and Welfare, Office of Education, 1960.

coordinating agencies were established in Wisconsin and Texas in 1955, and in Utah in 1959; voluntary bodies were created in Ohio in 1939, in California in 1945, and in Indiana in 1951. In 1955 the Michigan Legislature established a Legislative Study Commission on Higher Education and instructed it to investigate means of coordinating the efforts of the public institutions in meeting their present and future needs.[2]

The director of the survey of higher education made under the auspices of the Michigan Legislative Committee recommended that the legislature establish a board for the coordination of the state-controlled program of higher education in Michigan and that each institution under the coordinating agency's jurisdiction should have its own direct governing board, which should enjoy constitutional status. The proposed functions of the "master board" were outlined as follows: [3]

To collect, analyze, and report data concerning the programs, facilities, finances, and operation of all the state-controlled institutions of higher education.

To prepare for the Legislature and the state's fiscal authorities an annual estimate of the financial needs of each institution for operation and capital outlay, this report to include both the amount requested by the institution and the sum recommended by the coordinating board.

To advise the Legislature and other governmental authorities on all policy matters concerning the development and operation of higher education in the state, including such matters as the creation of a new institution or the development of a significant new educational service.

To make continuing studies of the state's needs for higher education and of the effectiveness of its educational services.

[2] *The Final Report of the Survey of Higher Education in Michigan,* Michigan Legislative Study Committee on Higher Education, Lansing, September, 1958, p. 112.

[3] *Ibid.*, pp. 113–116.

To provide advice and counsel to the officers of the state's colleges and universities.

To make whatever audits might be necessary to ensure the accuracy and uniformity of the institutions' report to the coordinating board.

In general, state college and university presidents have opposed the creation of coordinating agencies in the form of superboards, and one of the purposes—although not the only one—in establishing voluntary coordinating bodies has been to ward off the formal kind. For example, presumably hoping to forestall legislative acceptance of the survey director's recommendation in Michigan, the presidents of the nine public institutions took steps to strengthen the Michigan Council of State College Presidents—which was organized in 1951 and which has made important studies since that time—with the intention of turning the council into a functioning coordinating agency.

It is clear that a greatly strengthened council is the only means of warding off for long a formal coordinating board or engender legislative confidence in the budget requests of the Michigan institutions. What one newspaper referred to as "a pitched battle between two major state universities" [4] erupted during the Legislature's debate over the institutions' requests for operating funds. At the spring, 1960, session an official of Wayne State University urged the lawmakers to increase its appropriation substantially over the previous amount on the ground that this amount was $236 per student less than that for the University of Michigan and Michigan State University. A representative of the University of Michigan publicly opposed the increase on the ground that Wayne's plea failed to recognize the differences in types of student bodies, quality and salaries of faculties, and the productivity of the staff in scholarship and research. The Wayne official promptly replied that "any implica-

[4] *Ann Arbor News,* March 30, 1960.

tion that students attending WSU should be satisfied with less than the best is an indication that its students are second class citizens."

The two institutions, sensing that this interchange had benefited neither, later issued a joint statement emphasizing their agreement that both universities needed substantially larger appropriations and that their long history of close cooperation would continue.[5] However, the statement was issued only after demands had been made in the Legislature for a means of providing objective data on student costs, space utilization, and educational and research programs on the basis of which equitable appropriations could be made.

The Michigan Council of State College Presidents quickly announced that it would appoint a professional officer to supply essential information, to carry on research into the state's educational needs, and to serve as a liaison between the institutions and the Legislature in budget negotiations. But some members of the Legislature declared that it should appoint its own budgetary fact finder, whatever the Council of State College Presidents might do. Still other legislators asserted that the hassle had shown the soundness of the Russell proposal for a superboard and chancellor over the entire system of higher education.[6] As this was written, the legislative threat to appoint its own university fact finder had not been carried out; but the Council of State College Presidents had appointed an able professional director of studies.

The Michigan controversy is an example of the kind of public discord among higher institutions that makes either governmental intervention or formal coordination almost inevitable.

OBJECTIONS TO COORDINATION

What responsible university presidents and boards of trustees

[5] *Ibid.*, March 31, 1960.
[6] *Ibid.*, April 6, 7, 13; March 30, 1960.

most fear in formal coordination is the loss of the university's rightful independence. It has been asserted that all state universities which have attained eminence enjoy constitutional autonomy and that none of these institutions has been subjected to control by a master coordinating board. Eloquent appeals have been made to protect this autonomy and to maintain, in the words of President J. L. Morrill of the University of Minnesota, "the primacy of the state university in public higher education."

Morrill stated that he feared the newer "super-fiscal-coordinating board" which, while supposedly established to attain efficiency and economy, is actually created for the sole purpose of holding down state appropriations for higher education and usurping the authority of university boards of trustees. He saw in the operation of the formal coordinating agency a leveling process in which the weaker institutions would be strengthened and the more distinguished ones weakened. He likewise feared the invasion of constitutional autonomy by governors and state budget officers, leading to the ultimate "down-grading of the primacy of the state university" that had been built over the years by enlightened leadership and the devotion of eminent scholars and scientists.[7]

Morrill conceded that there would and should be a wider geographical dispersion of educational opportunity, accomplished in part by the establishment of new institutions. This was not the source of his concern. He considered what he called a "horizontal dispersion" of education at the undergraduate level in liberal studies, teacher education, and preprofessional curricula to be inevitable. But he warned that the "vertical divisibility" of the arduously achieved distinction of the university in science, scholarship, and research would be a "calamity of public policy and educational effectiveness."[8]

[7] J. L. Morrill, "The Place and Primacy of the State University in Public Higher Education," *Transactions and Proceedings of the National Association of State Universities in the United States of America*, vol. 56, 1958.
[8] *Ibid.*

This alarm over the consequences of dividing among too many institutions the total financial effort that can be mustered to support the research and scholarship that are the distinctive responsibilities of a major university is no idle fear. We as a people have the resources to finance a reasonably adequate program of higher education; but no state can afford the luxury of unnecessary duplication of educational opportunities, such as offering specialized, professional, or graduate curricula in more institutions than required to meet generously the demonstrated needs of the state or region and to make an appropriate contribution to the nation's supply of highly educated manpower. Neither can many states afford the luxury of turning all their public colleges into universities offering doctoral degrees in many fields, shouldering vast outlays for personnel and equipment. Even in wealthier states, the alternative to sensible allocation of responsibilities and the safeguarding of high quality is educational enfeeblement. One need not look far to see what happens to higher institutions when the support is thinly spread. The absence of quality is conspicuous.

But how is educational quality to be protected? How are unwarranted expansion and empire building to be checked? How are "vertical divisibility" and unnecessary duplication of high-level specialized, professional, and graduate programs to be avoided? Surely not by unilateral, sometimes chaotic action of single institutions. Surely not without concerted planning and coordinated effort among the public higher institutions of a state. How are the diverse needs of students and of society to be met? Surely not by all institutions struggling to be alike instead of performing distinctive functions. How is the primacy of the state university to be maintained? Surely not by trying to serve every student and every need instead of concentrating on its distinctive mission in the higher realms of scholarship, research, and service.

It is difficult to see how formal coordination would promote "vertical divisibility" of the university's functions, as President Morrill has implied. Formal coordinating agencies have been reasonably successful in the allocation of new programs to the institutions in their systems and in the preservation of traditional functions of graduate and professional education for the state university and the land-grant college.[9] The university's distinctive functions are much more likely to be dispersed and duplicated, and their quality attenuated, in an uncoordinated system.

COORDINATION IS INESCAPABLE

One can scarcely disagree with the President's Committee on Education beyond the High School, which asserted that although strenuous efforts will produce enlarged support for higher education, it will be insufficient to meet every need in full measure; therefore, it is essential to plan comprehensively, to establish and adhere to priorities, and to coordinate better the efforts of neighboring institutions.[10]

Swelling enrollments, mounting budgets, competition for funds among public services, and the establishment of new institutions would seem to make some kind of coordination inescapable. When the motivation for coordination is essentially negative, that is, when the main intent is to hold down expenditures,[11] to hold down institutions to the detriment of the state and its people, or to crush the initiative of the members of a system, then the effect of coordination will be unfortunate. When the motivation is positive and forward looking, when the purpose is to plan and support a diversified educational system of high quality and

[9] Glenny, *op. cit.*, p. 265.
[10] President's Committee on Education beyond the High School, *Second Report to the President*, Government Printing Office, Washington, 1957, p. 5.
[11] There is no evidence about whether the effect of formal coordination has been to reduce or increase expenditures for higher education; it would be extremely difficult to make such a determination.

to use financial resources efficiently, and when the greatest possible degree of freedom is left to individual institutions, the result should be constructive.

COORDINATION BY WHOM?

If coordination is inevitable, the first choice to be made is between coordination by external agencies—legislatures or state departments of finance—and by responsible educational bodies. Nearly everyone connected with the government and administration of higher education deplores the former. Legislatures may establish unnecessary new institutions of the wrong kinds or in the wrong places. They may, of course, do this in defiance of, or in spite of, the recommendations of coordinating agencies, but they are less likely to act in this fashion if the coordinating body has produced an orderly plan for the development of higher education in the state. In the absence of a responsible body to review the needs and financial requests of individual institutions, the state finance department may mediate among them, becoming in effect the coordinating agency. This function is far better performed by a lay or professional group created for the purpose. "There are many paths to effective coordination," said the Committee on Government and Higher Education, "and the choice of one depends on the special requirements of each state; but it is a certainty that if academic activities are not coordinated by the institutions themselves, the state will feel compelled to step in and do the job." [12]

The next choice, then, is, broadly, between a formal, legally established coordinating agency and a voluntary body. In the most complete analysis to date of the operation of coordinating boards, Glenny has appraised the effectiveness of both kinds of agencies. The results of his investigation are too extensive to be

[12] Committee on Government and Higher Education, *The Efficiency of Freedom*, Johns Hopkins Press, Baltimore, 1959, pp. 26–27.

repeated here, but some of his major conclusions may be summarized.

Glenny started with the assumption that the greatest single problem of coordination is how to avoid destroying the initiative, flexibility, and diversity that have been associated with autonomy. He stated that his data did not support the contention that formal coordinating boards have unduly standardized the institutions under their control; rather, except in a few instances, the central agencies have recognized the unique characteristics of the colleges and universities in the systems for which they are responsible. He said in conclusion that the fears of those in higher education that coordinated systems "impose uniformity" and "restrain initiative in many matters where uniformity is of secondary importance and initiative is vital to healthy institutional life" do not appear, on the basis of the evidence, to be well founded.[13]

AN APPRAISAL OF VOLUNTARY COORDINATION

The principal advantages of voluntary coordination, according to Glenny, are: [14]

The presidents themselves can limit coordinated activities to those of immediate concern either to the Legislature or the institutions.

Coordination is performed by persons directly responsible for, and intimately acquainted with, the institutions involved.

The dignity and responsibility traditionally associated with the presidency are maintained.

Each institution's historical autonomy is preserved.

By voluntary agreement to disclose unit cost studies, operating budgets, financial reports, and capital outlay schedules, the

[13] Glenny, *op. cit.*, p. 224.
[14] *Ibid.*, pp. 246–248.

suspicion and antagonism so often found among the state's institutions may be avoided. Although no central agency acts as judge or jury, a united front may be maintained in the Legislature.

Some of these advantages may turn into weaknesses from the point of view of the total needs of a state for higher education. Glenny summarized the limitations of voluntary coordination as follows:

Voluntary systems have a tendency to preserve the *status quo* —the relative position of the institutions in programs and in support—although new kinds of institutions may be needed or existing institutions should expand their services.

The participants in coordination are representatives of the institutions themselves—administrative officers or members of boards of trustees—and act without benefit of lay members representing the general public interest.[15]

Voluntary methods are unlikely to be effective in large and complex systems.

After discussing the possibility of strengthening voluntary agencies, Glenny concluded that even if the voluntary systems were improved in organization and operation, they could hardly be expected to serve state-wide interests and needs as effectively as formal coordinating agencies with legally assigned powers and responsibilities. "The primary motive of participants in voluntary systems is the welfare of individual institutions, not the system as a whole." [16]

Glenny severely criticized the voluntary agencies in Indiana and Ohio for preserving the *status quo*, for maintaining the relative positions of the institutions, and for failing to plan for new types of institutions or for development of established institutions to meet the needs of states which are increasingly urbanized

[15] The new voluntary Coordinating Council for Higher Education in California is an exception; it includes lay public representation.

[16] Glenny, *op. cit.*, p. 262.

and industrial. For example, he contended that Bowling Green and Kent state universities do not have the programs and financial support to meet the educational needs of the urban, industrialized centers of Toledo and Cleveland, near which they are situated.[17] Nevertheless, the record of accomplishment of the voluntary boards in Indiana and Ohio is significant. Glenny conceded that in these states cooperative relationships between public and private institutions stood out in sharp contrast to the hostility displayed among them in New York and to the mutual indifference he found in other states. He could not determine whether the rapport among the officers of the public institutions had set the tone for the entire state but concluded that their united front must have created for the public an "image of higher educational leadership committed to a common set of values cooperatively sought." [18]

Chambers recently made an even more favorable evaluation of the work of voluntary coordinating agencies and came out strongly against what he called the "coercion" of formal coordinating boards. He pointed out that not one of the nine top state-supported graduate schools is in a state having coordination of control. However, he did not offer this point as proof of the superiority of independence or voluntary coordination. In fact, he stated that it would almost be impossible to secure conclusive evidence of the relative superiority of the three methods of coordination he identified: voluntary coordination, compulsory coordination, and state-wide consolidation of operating control. He declared, however, that the trend is away from superimposed coordinating bodies.[19]

VOLUNTARY COORDINATION IN CALIFORNIA

In criticizing voluntary coordinating bodies, Glenny did not

[17] *Ibid.*, p. 251.
[18] *Ibid.*, p. 262.
[19] M. M. Chambers, "Voluntary Statewide Coordination in Public

spare the arrangement then operating in California, the Liaison Committee, composed of the chief executive officer and four members each of the governing boards of the University of California and the state colleges. Each system supplied a specialist in higher education, and these two persons—known as the Joint Staff—served as the principal professional staff for the Liaison Committee. The members of the Joint Staff were thus accredited to the participants rather than directly to the coordinating agency itself—yet the record shows that they maintained a remarkably objective point of view. The Liaison Committee had no power. It made its recommendations to the two governing boards, which were free to accept or reject them.

Glenny granted that the Liaison Committee, through studies conducted by the Joint Staff, had produced more pertinent data for planning California's program of higher education than had been available in any other state. He concluded, too, that the Liaison Committee had delineated the functions of the two systems and had supported the development of new institutions, new programs, and educational opportunities.[20]

Dr. T. C. Holy, who served from 1952 to 1960 as the University of California's representative on the Joint Staff of the Liaison Committee, has submitted as evidence of the committee's effectiveness the fact that, of fifty-five major recommendations which it transmitted to the two governing boards between 1945 and 1959, fifty-four were approved by the Regents of the University and fifty-three by the State Board of Education (for the state colleges), and that of the eighteen recommendations requiring legislation, sixteen were acted upon.[21]

But Glenny insisted that the Liaison Committee often ignored

Higher Education," University of Michigan, Ann Arbor, 1961, pp. 58–60.

[20] Glenny, *op. cit.*, p. 258.

[21] T. C. Holy, "California's Master Plan for Higher Education, 1960–1975," *Journal of Higher Education*, vol. 32, pp. 9–16, January, 1961.

important issues and that the two governing boards had some-times changed, amended, or ignored the recommendations of the committee (which, of course, was their prerogative). He stated, furthermore, that even when the governing boards did take a position on such policies as differential functions and programs, these policies were sometimes ignored or effectively negated by the institutions. In other words, the voluntary coordinating body did not have explicit authority or direction to determine compliance with established policy and, of course, did not have the power to see that policy was faithfully carried out.

The *Restudy of the Needs of California in Higher Education* recommended that the plan of voluntary coordination should be continued but proposed that the Liaison Committee should be expanded to permit representation of the junior colleges and that the professional staff should be accredited to the Liaison Committee and directly responsible to it rather than to the participating parties. It did not recommend that public members be added to the Liaison Committee; later deadlocks in the committee showed that this was a serious omission.

The responsibilities of the Liaison Committee, which was to be only advisory and consultative, were outlined as follows. It should appraise the effectiveness with which policies adopted by these boards were implemented—in other words, it was proposed that the committee should conduct continually what the restudy report had done on an *ad hoc* basis: a survey of the needs, costs, efficiency, and effectiveness of higher education in the state. It was not, however, to usurp the authority of the cooperating boards; the autonomy which the boards possessed by law was to remain intact.[22]

But the restudy's recommendations for strengthening the coordinating machinery, modest as they were, and insufficient

---

[22] T. C. Holy, T. R. McConnell, and H. H. Semans, *A Restudy of the Needs of California in Higher Education,* California State Department of Education, Sacramento, 1955, pp. 297–298.

as later events might well have proved them to be, were not adopted. Whether strengthened coordinative machinery would have prevented it or not, disagreement between the state colleges and the university intensified. The unresolved issues culminated, as noted earlier, in pressure by the state colleges to give doctoral degrees. The impasse that ensued led the Legislature to direct the Liaison Committee to prepare a new master plan for the development of post-high-school education and for the effective coordination of the state's public higher institutions. (The fact that the Legislature turned again to the Liaison Committee has been given as evidence of the committee's success and prestige.) [23]

The survey team preparing a master plan for coordination and for constitutional definition of the functions of the university, the state colleges, and the junior colleges considered three major means of coordination: (1) a single governing board for both the state colleges and the university, (2) a superboard over the two governing boards then in existence,[24] and (3) a plan for voluntary coordination of two separate but autonomous governing boards.[25] The latter plan was recommended.

The survey team proposed that the Liaison Committee be replaced by a Coordinating Council for Higher Education composed of three representatives each from the university, the state college system, the junior colleges, and the private institutions. The university and the state colleges were each to be represented by its chief executive officer and two members from its governing board; the junior colleges, by a member of the State Board of Education or its executive officer, a representative of local junior college governing boards, and a representative of the local junior college administrators. The representatives of the independent institutions

[23] *Ibid.*

[24] The Regents of the University of California and the State Board of Education.

[25] The regents and a new governing board for the state colleges, the latter to have constitutional autonomy, comparable to that enjoyed by the regents.

were to be selected by agreement of the chief executive officers of the university and the state college system in consultation with the association or associations of private colleges and universities. Thus, the council was to be composed of both lay members (representing not the public at large but the governing boards) and executive officers.

The plan proposed that all members of the council be given a vote on all questions. However, action on a junior college matter would require affirmative votes by five of the nine junior college, state college, and university representatives. Effective action on substantive matters affecting the university and the state colleges would require affirmative votes by four of the six state college and university members. On procedural matters the voting arrangements would be determined by rule of the council. The proposed voting scheme sounds somewhat like that in the Security Council of the United Nations. Either the university or the state college system could exercise a veto on any material question affecting one or the other or both systems, and no balance of power was left to the representatives of the junior colleges or the private institutions, although their attitudes conceivably could influence the votes of the effective membership.

No "public members" of the council were provided for in the survey team's report. It was argued that lay membership would predominate (from the governing boards) and that no useful purpose would be served either by adding public members or by inserting a lay board above the two governing boards. To many critics, the failure to provide for public members was a serious deficiency in the proposed plan, and something like the Wisconsin plan for public members of its coordinating body seemed preferable.

The Wisconsin Coordinating Committee for Higher Education is composed of five representatives each from the Regents of the University of Wisconsin and the Board of Regents of the state colleges, plus the state superintendent of public instruction and four citizen members appointed by the governor with the advice and consent of the Senate. All members of the committee have voting power. If the past is an indication, there will be numerous occasions in California on which the university and state college representatives of the coordinating body will be unable to agree on fundamental issues. Without public members to break the deadlock, the proposed new Coordinating Council could be as ineffective as the old Liaison Committee sometimes was in arriving at constructive solutions. Since the proposed council was to be only an advisory body—with the power to accept, reject, or ignore its recommendations vested, as before, in the two governing boards acting independently—it would seem to have been both in the broad public interest and in the interest of higher education as a whole to place the balance of power in part in public members.

This, at any rate, was essentially the position taken by the Legislature. To the three representatives each from the University of California, the state colleges, the public junior colleges, and the private institutions, the Legislature added three public members to be appointed by the governor. Furthermore, the legislative act creating the Coordinating Council gave it the power to prescribe rules for the transaction of its own affairs, subject to the requirements that the votes of all representatives should be recorded, that effective action should require the affirmative vote of eight members, and that the affirmative votes of ten members should be necessary for the appointment or removal of the director (the council's chief professional staff member). Presumably, all members of the council will have an effective vote on all questions, whereas the survey team had proposed that on substantive matters affecting the university and the state colleges only the representatives of the two systems would have had an effective vote, and action would have required affirmative votes by four of the six state college and university representatives. The master plan survey team recommended that the creation, composition, and powers of the Coordinating Council be made a part of the state constitution by amendment. This the Legislature declined to do.

The new California plan, like the one suggested in the Restudy, provides for a professional staff directly responsible to the Co-ordinating Council. On the energy and effectiveness of this professional staff much of the hope for the success of the new voluntary coordinating mechanism must rest. Only on the basis of continuing studies of the needs of the state in higher education, of the effectiveness with which these needs are being met, and of means of meeting them more fully and more adequately can the council, the responsible governing boards, the faculties and administrative staffs, and the legislative and executive governmental agencies plan and conduct a coordinated, comprehensive state-wide program of education beyond the high school.

In establishing the Coordinating Council, the Legislature gave it the following functions, advisory to the governing boards of the institutions and to appropriate state officials:

To review the annual budgets and requests for capital outlay of the university and state college systems and to comment on the general level of support sought.

To interpret the functional differentiation among the publicly supported institutions, in the light of this differentiation to advise on programs appropriate to each system, and to submit to the governor and the Legislature within five days of the beginning of each general session recommendations for desirable changes, if any, in the functions and programs of the several segments of public higher education.

To make plans for the orderly growth of higher education and to make recommendations concerning the need for, and the location of, new facilities and programs.

In addition, the council was given the power to require the public institutions of higher education to submit data on costs, selection and retention of students, enrollments, plant capacities, and other matters necessary for effective planning and co-

ordination and was directed to furnish the governor and the
Legislature information they might request. The integrity and
competence with which the council discharges these responsibilities, together with its clarity and persuasiveness in communicating
its findings and recommendations to the Legislature, the public,
and the institutions themselves, will determine in large part its
ability to cope with the enormously complicated problems that
confront it.

The master plan survey team also proposed to include a broad
definition of the differential functions of the junior colleges,
the state colleges, and the University of California in its proposed
constitutional amendment. It was said that writing a statement of
functions into the constitution would, because of the difficulty
of amendment, bring a new era of stability to public higher education; establish legal sanctions for enforcement, which had been the
weakest link in the old coordinating machinery; and provide
a standard by which each segment of higher education could
determine which of its offerings was marginal or central to its
functions. However, the Legislature declined to accept the recommendation that a statement of differential functions be incorporated in the state constitution.

It is doubtful whether a definition of differential functions
should be incorporated in a state constitution. But the question
of what is appropriately included in a constitution is not the only
consideration here. Another question is whether, however worth-
while some stability in institutional pattern may be, it is desirable
to try to freeze the status of the members of a system or the
relationships between systems of colleges and universities. Although the tendency to duplication rather than distinctiveness
was criticized in Chapter V, it was also pointed out that differentiation is almost certain to be unstable and that there should be
some opportunity for passage from one kind or level or quality
of institution to another.

In any event, the confidence in constitutional security might have turned out to be illusory. Putting a definition of differential functions into the constitution may give it the force of law, but this would be of little value if the provision were so general—as in part the formulation of the master plan was—that it would be subject to frequent interpretation. As the California experience has shown, practice may subvert formal policy. Only sincere commitment to the principle of differential functions and effective coordination will make a voluntary system work. It remains to be seen how deeply serious this commitment is among the parties to coordination in California and how well it endures.

Although the Legislature declined to incorporate a statement of differential functions in the constitution, it did include in its enactment of a new division on higher education in the Education Code the essence of the statement proposed by the survey team. The relevant sections of the act are:

Junior Colleges

The public junior colleges shall continue to be a part of the public school system of this State. The State Board of Education shall prescribe minimum standards for the formation and operation of public junior colleges and exercise general supervision over public junior colleges.

Public junior colleges shall offer instruction through but not beyond the 14th grade level, which instruction may include, but shall not be limited to, programs in one or more of the following categories: (1) standard collegiate courses for transfer to higher institutions; (2) vocational and technical fields leading to employment; and (3) general or liberal arts courses. Studies in these fields may lead to the associate in arts or associate in science degree.

State Colleges

The primary function of the state colleges is the provision of instruction for undergraduate students and graduate students, through the master's degree, in the liberal arts and sciences, in applied fields and in the professions, including the teaching profession. Presently established two-year programs in agriculture are authorized, but other two-year programs shall be authorized only when mutually agreed upon by the Trustees of the State College System and the State Board of Education. The doctoral degree may be awarded jointly with the University of California.... Faculty research is authorized to the extent that it is consistent with the primary function of the state colleges and the facilities provided for that function.

University of California

The Legislature hereby finds and declares that the University of California is the primary state-supported academic agency for research.

The university may provide instruction in the liberal arts and sciences and in the professions, including the teaching profession. The university has exclusive jurisdiction in public higher education over instruction in the profession of law, and over graduate instruction in the professions of medicine, dentistry, veterinary medicine and architecture.

The university has the sole authority in public higher education to award the doctoral degree in all fields of learning, except that it may agree with the state colleges to award joint doctoral degrees in selected fields.

The university may make reasonable provision for the use of its library and research facilities by qualified members of the faculties of other institutions of public higher education in this State.

The plan for voluntary coordination in California stands in sharp contrast to a plan recently proposed, but not adopted, in Illinois. Reference has been made earlier to the complex educational situation in that state and to the legislative mandate to

the Illinois Commission of Higher Education to devise a plan
for "the unified administration of all the state-controlled institutions of higher education." The commission interpreted the
Legislature's intent as a plan for unified government rather than
unified administration. In its annual report for 1960,[26] the commission proposed legislation to create a Board of Higher Education of eleven members appointed by the governor, with the
advice and consent of the Senate, for overlapping terms of six
years. The board was to have the following sweeping powers
and duties:

A. To analyze the present and future aims, needs and requirements of higher education in the State of Illinois and,
with the assistance of the institutions of higher education
in the state, to formulate a continuing state-wide plan of
development.

B. To consider, approve or disapprove, the plans of all
state controlled institutions of higher education relative to
the establishment of schools or departments in any field of
instruction, research, or public service not theretofore included in the program of such institutions, and the establishment of additional programs, facilities and institutions, to
be controlled and supported by the State. The determination
of such Board in these matters shall be final.

C. To consider, revise and approve the budget requests
of all state controlled institutions of higher education and
to request from the General Assembly the total amounts,
as determined by said Board, to be appropriated for such
purposes; further, unless specifically directed otherwise by
the General Assembly, to allocate the operating funds appropriated by the General Assembly in the same proportion as
contained in the Board's recommendation thereto, and to
allocate the capital funds in accordance with priorities which

[26] Illinois Commission of Higher Education, *Annual Report, 1960,*
Chicago, 1961, pp. 19–22.

the Board shall determine. The budget requests shall be considered solely in such manner.

D. To cause to be made such audits, inventories, surveys, and evaluations of all state controlled and supported institutions of higher education as it believes necessary for the purpose of providing appropriate information to carry out the powers and duties of the Board.

The proposed legislation provided further that

All official relationships and communications between the General Assembly and its various committees and the state controlled institutions of higher education shall be carried on through the Board. No official or agent representing any state controlled institution of higher education shall appear before any committee of the General Assembly except upon invitation transmitted by or through this Board.

Dr. David D. Henry, president of the University of Illinois, and Mr. Kenneth E. Williamson, president of the Board of Trustees, issued a joint statement opposing the proposed legislation. In a memorandum submitted to the Commission of Higher Education some time before, Henry had stressed the importance of cooperative planning when he said:[27]

I believe that statewide planning for higher education is imperative. Institutional expansion without professional study of the needs of the State as a whole or of the potential contribution of all institutions supplying that need is unwise. Considering the needs of one geographical area outside of the context of the needs of the State as a whole is an in-

[27] David D. Henry, "Comments for the Illinois Commission of Higher Education on Procedures for a Study of the Management and Control of the State Universities in Illinois." (An extension of remarks made at a public meeting of the commission, Aug. 7, 1959, Chicago.)

efficient way to approach satisfying the total requirements of the State. New developments in higher education should be based on a broad view of what is required in the public service, upon facts rather than bias, and upon consultation rather than unilateral decision. Further, there must be adequate machinery for carrying out of interinstitutional actions.

On another occasion Henry had conceded that "the record on voluntary planning is not very good" and that "one institution moving in a competitive spirit and without regard for the welfare of the state as a whole, one 'empire builder,' can destroy cooperative relationships." But at the same time he warned:[28]

> While we may believe that state planning is inevitable and that sound state planning may indeed result in conserving the traditional role of the state university, in encouraging a prudent use of the state's resources, and in restoring an orderly pattern where there is now confusion of relationships, we must also take note of the parallel public concern with the question of enforced coordination of the state universities and other institutions. . . .
>
> A single board of control for the public institutions within a state is not a panacea, however. Experience with this mechanism is uneven among the states where it has been tried and at best it cannot deal adequately with the institutions outside its jurisdiction. Further, merely amalgamating boards of control or creating a "super board" does not automatically achieve the result desired among the institutions directly concerned. In the more complex institutions, particularly, there should also be carefully designed plans for integration of administration and of program and agree-

[28] David D. Henry, "The University's Relationships with Other Colleges and Universities," in Logan Wilson (ed.), *The State University*, University of Texas Press, Austin, Tex., 1959, pp. 8–9.

ment on general objectives. Without such integration, a
super-board plan may but transfer present confusion from
one arena to another. . . .

In facing these new developments, moreover, it must be
emphasized that coordination is a result, not a process. It
cannot be imposed. It does not arrive suddenly. It does not
come through edict or mandate. Effective state plans grow
out of the experience of institutions in working together.

In the joint statement referred to above, Henry and Williamson objected to the proposed coordinating board on the ground
that the board would possess "a concentration of authority and
power which could threaten the stability, integrity, and effectiveness of the state universities"; that the present three boards
of control would be reduced to the status of little more than
advisory committees—a board subordinate to another board for
final budget decisions would be unable to carry out its responsibilities; and that these boards would be prohibited from approaching the governor, the Legislature, or the people in dissent-
ing from a decision of the proposed Board of Higher Education.

The Legislature did not accept the Illinois Commission's proposals. Instead, it adopted a bill with the following provisions,
in part:[29]

A Board of Higher Education was created to consist of fifteen
members including eight appointed by the governor with the
advice and consent of the Senate, the chairmen of the boards
of trustees of the University of Illinois and Southern Illinois
University and the Teachers College board; an additional member of the three boards; and the superintendent of public instruction.

The Board of Higher Education was directed to analyze the
present and future aims, needs, and requirements of higher

[29] Illinois, 72nd General Assembly, House Bill no. 1591 in Senate,
1961.

education in the state; to prepare a master plan for the development, expansion, integration, coordination, and efficient utilization of the facilities for public higher education in teaching, research, and public service; to engage in a continuing evaluation and revision of the plan; and to submit to the General Assembly the legislation necessary for the implementation of the plan.

The three governing boards were enjoined from establishing any new unit of instruction, research, or public service (such as a college, school, division, institute, department or other unit not previously included, as well as a branch or campus) not approved by the Board of Higher Education.

The Board of Higher Education was directed to submit to the General Assembly, the governor, and other appropriate governmental agencies its analysis and recommendations concerning the budgets for operation and capital outlay proposed by the three governing boards.

The board was given access to all records of the institutions and governmental agencies (subject only to laws or regulations regarding confidentiality) that it deemed necessary to the discharge of its responsibilities.

The board was empowered to employ a professional staff. In its power to approve or disapprove a proposed new unit of instruction, research, or public service in the institutions under the three governing boards, the Illinois Board of Higher Education was given greater power than that possessed by the Coordinating Council in California, whose province in such matters is only advisory.

The debates and actions concerning coordination in the several states have made the basic issue clear: the choice between formal and voluntary bodies and procedures involves a balancing of values, and the values of independence, initiative, and responsibility weigh heavily in the quest for institutional excellence and integrity. The end to be gained is a *productive* compromise between the values of autonomy and coordination.

The writer is not yet ready to concede that voluntary coordination cannot meet the need for cooperative planning, definition of institutional roles and relationships, and integrity in carrying out agreements. Of one thing he is certain, however: if voluntary methods fail—and they will not have much time to prove their effectiveness—formal coordinating mechanisms are inevitable.

COORDINATION ABROAD:
ENGLISH TECHNICAL EDUCATION

One can often understand the educational problems of his own country better if he sees them against the background of educational conditions in other nations. In weighing the claims of institutional autonomy against the need for coordinated effort in higher education in the United States, it may be useful to look briefly at two attempts at coordination abroad—both in England. One is the reorganization of technical education, which has involved a degree of systematization which would be unacceptable in the United States. The other is the welding of the universities into a national system by the University Grants Committee, through which governmental support is channeled to the institutions. The University Grants Committee is not a device that would be applicable in the United States, either, but the effect on the independence of the British universities of its effort to fit them into a national scheme has something to say to us about the balance between autonomy and coordination.

It was suggested in the Introduction that external and internal forces will make a greater degree of *rationalization* necessary in American higher education. Perhaps the word "rationalization" is too strong. In any event, it was not used by any means in the tight sense in which British educational leaders have referred to the rationalization of further education (in this instance, technical education particularly) which overlaps the secondary schools at one extreme and the universities at the other. The need for systematizing technical education in England and Wales was said to have arisen because the technical colleges had attempted to meet an external demand for training and because their curricula sometimes reflected a principal's expansionist desires more than a need for additional courses. As a consequence, the colleges, with their haphazard structure, were thought to be unable to support new engineering programs at the university level. This, coupled with a severe shortage of highly qualified teachers of technology, was said to demand a rationalization of the entire system of technical training and also of technological education outside the universities.[30]

This rationalization, directed largely by the Ministry of Education with the assistance of advisory groups, has taken the form of a hierarchical organization of four groups of technical institutions: local colleges, area colleges, regional colleges, and colleges of advanced technology.[31] The number of institutions of each type becomes progressively smaller the more centralized and advanced the colleges become—300, 170, 22, and 9.

In the local colleges, part-time and evening work predominates. Most of it is elementary, none extending beyond the level of the Ordinary National Certificate (roughly the technical level). In the area colleges, the work is also mainly part-time but it takes the student beyond the level attained in the local colleges to the Higher National Certificate or, for the relatively small number of full-time or "sandwich" students,[32] the Higher National Diploma.

The teaching in the regional colleges, however, is more advanced. The great majority of the work is beyond the Ordinary National Certificate, and some of those colleges have courses ap-

[30] A. A. Part, "Education for Industry and Commerce," *Journal of the Royal Society of Arts,* vol. 108, pp. 16–29, December, 1959.
[31] There are also national colleges in fields in which the need for personnel is not large or in which the industries are widely dispersed.
[32] Those who alternate full-time schooling with full-time in industry.

proved for the university level Diploma in Technology as well as the Higher National Diploma. A large part of the work is done in full-time or sandwich courses, a distinguishing feature of the regional institution.

The capstone of the system is the college of advanced technology, which is required to divest itself of all its elementary instruction and concentrate exclusively on work at the undergraduate and postgraduate levels leading to the Diploma in Technology or to Membership of the College of Technologists.

Kinds and standards of courses in the four types of colleges are differentially selective. One level of college may feed another; thus a student who finishes a local college may, if he has the requisite ability, go on to a regional college or college of advanced technology, although students with the proper background are more likely to enter such colleges directly. The two means of entry to the colleges of advanced technology are completion of the grammar school or an equivalent course at one of the other types of technical colleges.

The scheme also provides for movement of colleges from one category to another. Since the system was established, certain area colleges have become regional institutions and one regional college has been designated as a new college of advanced technology.[33]

Not all parties have approved of this rationalization. Some colleges which had developed a substantial amount of advanced work were unhappy when they were not made colleges of advanced technology, even though some of their courses were approved for the Diploma in Technology. Also, some local and area colleges were disgruntled either at having to turn over their advanced work to other colleges or at not being permitted to extend their offering upwards. Not surprisingly, therefore, the Ministry of Education was subjected to political and other pres-

---

[33] This account of the system is taken from the article by A. A. Part and from P. F. R. Venables, "Technical Education," *Journal of the Royal Society of Arts*, vol. 108, pp. 30–47, December, 1959.

sures when setting up the system, but although some compromises admittedly were made, on the whole the plan was developed rationally and straightforwardly.

Although the plan of technical education (for England and Wales) is a national one, the colleges are still under the immediate control of local education authorities, and are encouraged to adapt their programs to local, area, regional, and national needs as may be appropriate. There are planning and coordinating bodies, as well, in the form of regional advisory councils; these aid in the orderly development of the colleges in their sections of the country by advising on the courses which the colleges propose to offer. The master coordinator, however, is the Ministry of Education, which supplies from 60 to 75 per cent of the financial support of the colleges and is able to exercise control over their programs and their development.

No such neat and orderly system will develop in the United States. First, the size and complexity of the country itself makes the problem of educational planning and coordination vastly more complicated than in Britain. Second, the control of secondary and technical education is more centralized in England than in the United States, where the tradition of local control, and in many states of predominantly local support, of secondary education is deeply entrenched. In most states, too, the junior colleges are locally controlled and for the most part locally supported,with little supervision from above. The responsibility for higher education beyond the junior colleges is even more widely dispersed. Nothing as highly articulated as the English system of technical education is likely to emerge here, for it requires too great a sacrifice of institutional self-determination.

UNIVERSITY COORDINATION IN ENGLAND

The English experience in fitting the universities into a national pattern of development has more to tell us about the compromise between complete independence and a high degree of integration.

After an intensive analysis of the historical and contemporary relations between the universities and the state in Britain, and particularly of the extent to which the universities had surrendered their independence in the national service, an American political scientist, Berdahl, came to the conclusion that "the universities, all privately founded and until recent years largely self-financed, formerly governed themselves in splendid isolation from one another and the state; now, however, they have become in effect part of an articulated national system of higher education, each still self-governing but strongly influenced by national policies in many of its decisions, regarding curricula, faculty, student body, capital plant, and research, and each currently receiving an amount near the national average of three-fourths of its annual income from the state funds." [34]

Berdahl quoted Churchill's Chancellor of the Exchequer as admonishing the universities in 1944–1945 "to regard themselves no longer as isolated units, but rather as parts of an articulated whole [whose] activities must be coordinated in the interests of efficiency and economy of effort" and as placing this responsibility upon the universities themselves through the appropriate agencies of cooperation. Berdahl concluded, however, that although the universities, through such agencies as the Committee of Vice-Chancellors and Principals, have voluntarily engaged in many useful undertakings, it is now generally agreed that in its major aspects coordination is the responsibility of the state.[35]

The principal instrument by which the British universities have been welded into a national system is the University Grants Committee, an arm of the state Treasury (with membership drawn largely from the academic community) which is responsible for submitting to Parliament the financial needs of the uni-

[34] R. O. Berdahl, *British Universities and the State*, University of California Publications in Political Science, vol. 7, University of California Press, Berkeley, Calif., 1959, p. 2.
[35] *Ibid.*, p. 188.

versities and for distributing the state appropriations among them. Berdahl stated that even if the universities had been wealthy enough not to need state subsidies, the Treasury grants would have had to be invented, "for no one can seriously contend ... that the contemporary state would be able to forego efforts to integrate their activities into the framework of national planning." [36]

The University Grants Committee, in pursuance of its responsibility for ensuring that the universities "are fully adequate to national needs," draws up its requests for Treasury support after extensive consultation, first of all with the universities themselves. The committee is also in constant touch with the branches of government which employ professional personnel and it enjoys the advice of the professional societies and the scholarly associations. It takes advantage of the reports of special commissions or committees of inquiry (such as those on agricultural, veterinary, dental, and medical education in the universities; on the need for expansion in Oriental, African, East European, and Slavic studies; on the development of social and economic research; and on the necessity for dramatic expansion in the number of students in science, technology, and the arts).

On the basis of such extensive consultation and investigation, the committee submits to the Chancellor of the Exchequer its yearly estimates for capital outlay and its quinquennial requests for university operation and development. Until 1952, in order to assure that funds allocated to universities for special developments were used for these purposes, the committee made earmarked grants, in distinction to the "block" grants for the remainder of university support.

However, there were two sides to this question, illustrated by the contention of a vice-chancellor of Oxford that the university had been offered too much money for the social sciences and by the contrary assertion of a distinguished social scientist that the

[36] *Ibid.*, p. 187.

universities' negative attitude toward the social sciences had been disastrous for these disciplines and that the "U.G.C. should ... accept some responsibility for making the universities do the right things, even where the reactionary elements largely at the head of them are strongly opposed." [37]

After a careful and extensive analysis of the extent to which the intervention of the University Grants Committee in the affairs of the universities had compromised their independence, Berdahl asserted that thus far the committee had succeeded in its "delicate task," which was to enable the universities to make a maximum contribution to the national interest while holding the inevitable decline in autonomy to the minimum, not only to preserve academic freedom but also to serve the long-range public interest of properly limiting the power of the state.[38] Berdahl conceded that the real test was still to come, however, because the state's limited goals for the universities had allowed them to cooperate voluntarily and because the delicate balance between university autonomy and national educational planning depended on presently prevailing favorable conditions which might not persist.[39]

The United States is so vast and complex in comparison to Britain that a truly national system of higher education will hardly develop in this country. The reference to the coordinating effort of the British University Grants Committee was not intended to imply that we should attempt to coordinate higher education in the United States on a national scale. We will do well to devise orderly arrangements for higher education at the state level.[40] At this level, however, although to transpose its proce-

[37] *Ibid.*, p. 147.
[38] *Ibid.*, p. 3.
[39] *Ibid.*, p. 166.
[40] Even at the national level, however, some coordination takes place through such agencies as the National Science Foundation, which, in distributing its research funds, takes national needs as well as institutional qualifications into account. As Federal support of higher edu-

dures would be manifestly unwise or even impossible, the experience of the University Grants Committee is relevant. It has shown that under favorable conditions it is possible to plan the development of higher education comprehensively and to coordinate the efforts of individual institutions in meeting the objectives of a broad program without unduly sacrificing the integrity, identity, initiative, and essential independence of the parts of the system. We should be able to devise mechanisms and methods for accomplishing the same goals that are appropriate to our own social, economic, and educational conditions.

IN CONCLUSION

Effective coordination sometimes undeniably entails restraint, but if the results of coordination are mainly negative they will be unfortunate. The great need in public higher education is for constructive, collaborative, and comprehensive planning, and for purposeful sharing, as well as purposeful division, of responsibilities. If colleges and universities are to meet future needs, they will have to engage in extensive experimentation and encourage fruitful innovation. In appraising old purposes and setting new goals, and in discovering better means of attaining educational objectives, room for imagination and innovation is abundant, and opportunity for improving the educational process all along the line is plentiful. The United States should even have room for sensible competition between systems of colleges or individual institutions; coordination should not be so rigid as to eliminate elasticity in the pattern of higher education.

---

cation grows—as it will—we may expect a still greater degree of planning on a national scale.

IX THE INDIVIDUAL STUDENT
AND THE SYSTEM

Although even in a democracy it is not necessary for every student to have access to every kind of institution, he should not encounter unreasonable barriers to transfer from one kind or level of institution to another. No ultimate educational or professional opportunity should be closed to a student at an early point in his schooling. A flexible educational system must include a succession of choice points at which a student may go in one of two or more directions—at which, for example, he may choose among different institutions or specialties, or transfer from one college or university to another.

EXAMPLE OF AN INFLEXIBLE SYSTEM

An educational system in which, for all practical purposes, choice at an early age determines the student's ultimate educational and vocational destiny is not flexible. Such is the English system, in which the destiny of most students is determined by an examination when he is about eleven years old or slightly older.

The Education Act of 1944 gave England three types of secondary schools: the traditional grammar schools, the new modern schools, and the new technical schools (which have developed slowly and are still relatively few in number). The examination at eleven-plus is the basis of distributing students among these institutions. About 20 per cent of the age group are admitted to the grammar schools, which—except for the so-called public or independent schools, "multilateral schools," and the new comprehensive secondary schools (to be discussed later) and in some instances the technical secondary schools—are the avenues to the university. Thus, university admission and entry into a wide range of occupations are contingent upon selection for particular kinds of schools or programs.

The system of parallel but separate secondary schools has been attacked as undemocratic, as a convenient means of perpetuating a stratified society. True, since the reform of 1944, selection for the grammar schools has been based on the child's aptitude and achievement, and not, as it frequently had been before, on his family's ability to pay tuition. But the fortunate minority who gain admission win not only educational preference but also social standing. It is a blow to a family's social status if its child fails to meet grammar school standard and a boost to another's if its son or daughter is admitted. Theoretically, the modern secondary schools were to be given "parity of esteem," which, as might have been expected, proved to be an unattainable social goal. Grammar school selection on the basis of intellectual ability rather than ability to pay was a profound innovation; it introduced social mobility but also maintained a stratified school system.

The parallel school system has been attacked also on the ground that classification on the basis of the eleven-plus examination is fallible, especially in a certain range of performance. Studies have shown that assignment to the modern secondary school frequently results in misplacements and waste of talent. It has been estimated, for example, that if a hundred students are tested at age eleven, and twenty of them are selected for grammar school, five to seven will be admitted who should not be, and five to seven excluded who should be selected.[1] It has been contended that it would not be a tragedy for a student capable of satisfactory grammar school work to be denied admission and sent instead to a modern secondary school, because it is possible to transfer from modern schools to grammar schools if the misplacement is discovered early enough. In practice, however, this shift occurs very infrequently.

One of the principal members of the staff of the Ministry of Education who, like many of his colleagues, favors the segregated school system, gave the writer the transfer argument in supporting separate schools. When pressed, however, he admitted that not more than 2 per cent of the students who had entered other schools later transferred to grammar schools—a number appreciably smaller than the number of children originally misassigned.

The recognition of such considerations lent strong impetus to a postwar movement to establish comprehensive secondary schools, which, however, are still not numerous. The comprehensive system avoids the stigma of assignment to socially less preferred schools, although students may be placed in ability groups and assigned to various curricular "streams." But all students take some common subjects in the earlier years and participate in a wide range of school activities. With internal differentiation goes progressive appraisal of achievement and ability and easier transfer from one curriculum to another when this is desirable.[2]

[1] These data are based on passing of the general certificate of education at the ordinary level. *Observer*, Feb. 22, 1960.

[2] Some city school systems in England which have maintained separate schools have adopted a system of progressive selection by reviewing a child's original assignment year by year and arranging for transfer from one school to another in appropriate cases.

A FLEXIBLE SYSTEM KEEPS
ALTERNATIVES OPEN

The English system still has far to go in attaining the flexibility and scope of the American educational scheme, which has been characterized as follows by Robert Gordon Sproul:[3]

The development of American education has been motivated from the beginning by a desire to provide equality of opportunity for all youth and not by the concept of preparing a limited number of the supposedly best minds for a few traditional professions, but by offering a wide range of choices over a long period of time, and postponement of a decision as to a college career to a relatively late date. Consequently, there has developed in the United States a more or less flexible arrangement of schools and colleges which permits, although it does not always achieve, guidance of students in the studies appropriate to their talents and interests, as these may be discovered almost anywhere along the line from elementary school to university, and into types of institutions that are able to stretch, but not to snap, the student's capacity to learn. Coupled with the great variety of courses and curricula characteristic of American universities, and especially the land-grant colleges, this means, of course, that there are fewer roadblocks to late choices.

Although the institutions of the California system perform different functions, as explained earlier, they have some responsibilities in common. For example, all three groups of public institutions provide general, liberal, and preprofessional education. Therefore, a student who ultimately may enter the graduate school or one of the professional schools of the University of

[3] R. G. Sproul, "Many Millions More," *Educational Record*, vol. 39, pp. 97–107, April, 1958.

California may begin his higher education in a junior college and transfer to one of the state colleges for a baccalaureate degree. Such student mobility among the institutions of a differentiated system is essential if educational opportunity for all students is to be limited only by their aptitude and accomplishment.

Coupled with successive choice points should be the opportunity, within reasonable limits, to repair deficiencies as a means of meeting higher, or at least different, standards of admission to institutions or curricula. Thus, a student who, because of inadequate counseling or because of a change in educational objective, failed to take enough mathematics in high school should be given the chance to make up this deficiency for admission to an engineering school. California high school graduates not eligible for admission to the University of California because of unsatisfactory scholarship or failure to take the necessary pattern of high school subjects may qualify in the junior college by taking an appropriate program and meeting the scholastic standard required for transfer to the university with advanced standing.

THE PRICE OF FLEXIBILITY

The price that must be paid for such flexibility is an indistinct line between one stage of higher education and the next, for example, between secondary and higher education. Some critics of American education would like to duplicate in this country the sharp separation of secondary and university schooling which characterizes both English and Continental education. The Continental and English universities generally assume that the secondary school graduate has completed his formal general education and is prepared to embark on his specialized or professional studies immediately.[4]

[4] There is one exception among the English universities. The University College of North Staffordshire, reacting to the curtailment of general education and the beginning of specialization in the sixth form

In the United States, on the other hand, colleges and universities usually assume that the high school student's general education is insufficient and that he should continue it during a part of, and in some institutions throughout, his college program. The student may also strengthen his specific preparation for specialized work after he enters college.

Many students change their educational and vocational goals, not only during high school or between high school and college, but also after entering college. As noted previously, the Center for the Study of Higher Education has been studying the college careers of an exceptionally able group of students, winners and runners-up in the 1956 National Merit Scholarship Corporation competition. The Center has data on changes in intended fields of specialization between the summer before college entrance and the end of the sophomore year for 525 NMSC men. A distinction was made between a major change, defined as a shift to an unrelated field, as from mathematics to history, and a minor change, defined as a shift to a closely related field.

In all, 245 students, or 40 per cent, made changes—more than 25 per cent a major change, and an additional 15 per cent a minor change. The largest number of changes was made by students who had originally chosen to concentrate in the humanities or the social sciences, the next largest number by those in the natural sciences and mathematics, and the fewest by those in engineering; 41 students changed twice, nearly half shifting to fields unrelated to their original choices. The prevalence of changes in educational and vocational choice shows clearly the need for organizational flexibility in higher education.[5]

---

of the grammar school, requires four rather than three years for the degree and devotes the first year to a program of general education for all students.

[5] J. R. Warren, "Change in College Field of Study as a Function of Discrepancy between Self-concept and Expected Occupational Role," unpublished doctoral dissertation, University of California, Berkeley, 1959.

Nevertheless, flexibility can breed inefficiency. For example, a student may spend valuable time repairing deficiencies that adequate counseling would have enabled him to avoid. Conant has recommended that, with few exceptions, students in the upper 15 per cent in ability should take four years of mathematics in high school. The writer would be inclined to consider a greater number of exceptions, especially for students strongly drawn to the humanities or the arts, but it is clear that a mathematical background is now essential for scholarship and research in the behavioral as well as the natural sciences.

Blurring the line between secondary and higher education makes possible the deepening and widening of general education and keeps educational alternatives open for a longer time. But it also permits undue procrastination in making educational and vocational decisions. For many students, too, it may mean wasting time in repetitive and undemanding courses. Thus, what in one respect is a flexible system may in another become a wasteful one.

ACCOMPLISHMENT SHOULD DETERMINE INDIVIDUAL PROGRESS

A flexible system should stimulate a student to move through it at a rate commensurate with his capacity and achievement. We have only begun to encourage this, although some of the ways to go about it have been demonstrated for a quarter century.

More than twenty-five years ago a study made at the University of Buffalo showed that high school and college curricula greatly overlapped.[6] Subsequently, the university, to save the

[6] E. S. Jones (ed.), *Studies in the Articulation of High School and College,* University of Buffalo Studies, vol. 9, 1934, and vol. 13, 1937, Buffalo.

time of capable students, announced a program of advanced standing based on examinations on university level courses in the College of Arts and Sciences. The university supplied syllabuses of certain courses in the college to interested high school teachers and students. The latter were encouraged to do the reading for the college courses and to take an examination prepared at the university, which, if passed, would give them college credit. An evaluation of this program conducted long after its inauguration showed that it had been highly successful.

When compared with a control group, students who took the "anticipatory examinations" were more likely to complete the requirements for the baccalaureate degree; they made comparable grades in the junior and senior divisions of the college; and they made almost equivalent scores on the advanced and general profile tests of the Graduate Record Examination. Furthermore, the social activities of the two groups were similar, except that fewer of the "anticipatory" group joined fraternities or participated in athletics.[7]

At about the time the Buffalo studies began, Cornell College announced an experiment in early admission. Students of outstanding academic aptitude who had made an exceptional high school record and who were deemed to be socially and emotionally mature enough to adjust satisfactorily to the college environment were admitted at the end of the eleventh grade. Not many students entered under the experiment, but those who did were uniformly successful and, as a group, superior in academic accomplishment. There were no cases of social or emotional stress.[8]

Other studies and projects emphasized the importance of advancing students in accordance with their development, but to little general effect in American higher education. Few institu-

[7] E. S. Jones and G. K. Ortner, *College Credit by Examination*, University of Buffalo Studies, vol. 21, no. 3, Buffalo, January, 1954.

[8] T. R. McConnell, "Educational Articulation," *Journal of Higher Education*, vol. 5, pp. 253–258, May, 1934.

tions adjusted their machinery to permit students to escape what Aydelotte called "the academic lockstep." The inertia of higher education is hard to break.

After a quarter century of inaction, *General Education in School and College* appeared,[9] exposing the duplication between high school and college in the halls of the Ivy League. The report revealed that many freshman courses at Harvard, Yale, and Princeton duplicated the preparatory work of three private New England secondary schools, Andover, Exeter, and Lawrenceville.

This study, which was supported by the Fund for the Advancement of Education, led the Fund to give large-scale support to two projects—early admission to college and admission with advanced standing. In the first, qualified students were financially assisted to attend colleges and universities after completing the tenth or eleventh grade. A group of institutions was also given large-scale assistance to develop college level syllabuses in several fields, to prepare examinations in these courses, and to cooperate with secondary schools in encouraging high school students to prepare for these examinations. On the basis of these examinations, they might be given advanced standing or course credit in the colleges and universities they attended.

These projects, too, were highly successful. In general, the younger entrants did even better college work than the regular students with whom they were compared and were more likely to attend graduate school; they were socially well adjusted and emotionally stable; and they engaged in extracurricular activities at least as extensively as their classmates. They testified that early admission to college had freed them from "the boredom and frustration of an unchallenging high school environment, gave them new intellectual momentum, and enhanced their social and

[9] *General Education in School and College,* (committee report by members of the faculties of Andover, Exeter, Lawrenceville, Harvard, Princeton, and Yale), Harvard University Press, Cambridge, Mass., 1952.

emotional maturation." Through the other project, a large number of students attained advanced standing with or without credit.[10] This project has now become a regular program of the College Entrance Examination Board.

A growing number of institutions are encouraging students to take advantage of advanced standing examinations, and the number of examinations administered by the College Board has grown rapidly. In 1961, 10,531 candidates took 14,158 examinations; the students came from 890 schools and entered 567 colleges.[11] Nevertheless, the total number is still too small. The machinery of units and credits still paces too many students' progress through the system.

A comprehensive and flexible plan of higher education requires periodic assessment of individual aptitudes, interests, and attainments; differentiation of educational opportunities; recurrent efforts to pair students and institutions or students and curricula; and movement through the system on the basis of accomplishment rather than of time served.

DIFFICULTIES IN PAIRING STUDENTS
AND INSTITUTIONS OR CURRICULA

Flexibility is essential in the development of American higher education for still another reason. Although the arrangements for post-high-school education should be organized in more orderly fashion, we do not yet know enough about careers, student characteristics, and the character of college environments to establish a tidy array of differentiated institutions and to enable

[10] *Bridging the Gap between School and College,* (evaluation report no. 1), Fund for the Advancement of Education, New York, 1953. *They Went to College Early,* (evaluation report no. 2), Fund for the Advancement of Education, New York, 1957.

[11] *Advanced Placement News Letter,* College Entrance Examination Board, New York, February, 1961.

students to distribute themselves among them according to their individual traits. Neither do we know enough at this stage to pair students and specialized curricula with great precision.

We know too little, first of all, about the activities for which youths and adults need to be trained. For example, we know that physicians must be trained, but medicine is an enormously varied occupation; physicians do many different things and need different kinds, or at least different emphases, of preparation. Yet the specifications for this variety have not been written.

Second, we are still relatively ignorant about the demands that different careers make on human abilities and dispositions. For example, we have only just begun to study objectively the differences in abilities and aptitudes, interests and attitudes, and other personality characteristics that differentiate one specialist from another or that distinguish the teacher, researcher, or theoretician from the practitioner in these specialties. To use physicians as examples again, a small beginning in the exploration of these differential characteristics has been made cooperatively by the Center for the Study of Higher Education and the research division of the Association of American Medical Colleges. This was a study of the diversity in psychological characteristics of medical school seniors planning to enter various specialties. It was discovered that there was a full standard deviation in Medical College Aptitude Test scores between the group expecting to go into general practice and the one planning to enter psychiatry; further, there were differences among the specialty groups on the Allport-Vernon-Lindzey scales and on the scales of the Edwards Personal Preference Schedule. These differences are too complicated to summarize here—in fact, they are too complicated in the present stage of our analysis to allow meaningful interpretation or practical use. Furthermore, we do not know whether the characteristics of students planning to enter the various specialties correspond with those of practitioners, much less successful practitioners, in the same medical fields. But at least a beginning has been made on the differential psychological analysis of the several kinds of medical practice and of medical teaching and research.[12] On page 70 we mentioned an analysis of engineering tasks which yielded five principal, partly overlapping clusters of activities—research and development, production and sales, technical services, design, and supervision and administration. We also mentioned on page 70 a related study which showed that persons performing these relatively distinct engineering tasks differed in some psychological characteristics.

The Center has been exploring the personality characteristics of various groups of students intending to major in different academic fields. It has found in studies of National Merit Scholarship freshmen and of freshmen at the California Institute of Technology that those intending to major in mathematics and physics had a different orientation toward learning from those who intended to major in engineering. The differences were statistically significant in measures of thinking introversion (interest in ideas as such), theoretical and aesthetic orientation, and social maturity—the latter a test in which authoritarianism is a large component. Differences, although not statistically significant, were also observed on tests of complexity and originality. Scores on the same scales differentiated even more strongly among National Merit Scholarship groups intending to major in the social sciences, the humanities, and education.[13] A recent summary of comparable investigations showed that students majoring

[12] H. H. Gee, "Differential Characteristics of Student Bodies: Implications for the Study of Medical Education," in T. R. McConnell (ed.), *Selection and Educational Differentiation*, Field Service Center and Center for the Study of Higher Education, University of California, Berkeley, 1960.

[13] P. Heist and H. Webster, "Differential Characteristics of Student Bodies: Implications for Selection and the Study of Undergraduates," in *ibid.*, pp. 91–106.

in various academic fields may be different as groups, not only in general scholastic aptitude, but also in attitudes and personality characteristics.

But this kind of information, important as it is, does not provide an easy means of guiding students into major fields or professional careers. Guiding a student into a major for which he is temperamentally fitted or in which he may make the highest academic record may not be best for his personal development. From the latter point of view, it may be wiser to encourage the student to concentrate in a field in which he would not make a high academic record.[14] It is appropriate to ask whether the purpose of a liberal education is to confirm people in what they are or to offer them new experiences which could change their attitudes.

Until we discover far more about the nature of educational fields and vocational careers and about the human traits that are necessary for success in them, until we learn more about the effect which different fields of study may have on the development of interests, attitudes, and intellectual dispositions, in fact, on the deeper aspects of the personality, we will be handicapped in helping students to choose appropriate institutions or in aiding them to choose suitable curricula.

One difficulty in this task is our lack of a secure basis for unveiling the wide spectrum of human talents and temperaments. We have rough methods of assessing a student's general academic aptitude, but we have made only limited progress in measuring special aptitudes or in predicting differential academic achievement. With our present instruments we could, if we wished, do a fairly good job of stratifying institutions by the level of academic ability of their entrants, and, as Wriston has proposed,

---

[14] C. Bereiter and M. B. Freedman, "Fields of Study and People in Them," chapter prepared for N. Sanford (ed.), *The American College: A Psychological and Social Interpretation of the Higher Learning.* John Wiley & Sons, Inc., New York, (in press.)

we could greatly reduce the spread of ability in student bodies if we decided this would be wise. But if we made a university homogeneous in general academic ability, the institution might still be variable in other characteristics—interests and motivation, attitudes and values, intellectual bents and dispositions which are related in subtle ways to the satisfactions students get from studies, the field of their specialization, and their careers. We still know very little of the way in which these attributes dispose a student to develop in certain ways or inhibit his growth in other directions. Fortunately, there has been an upsurge of interest in this problem; significant studies are under way of the changes in students during the college years and of the individual characteristics and social forces contributing to development or stagnation. Thus, the Center is investigating student development intensively at Antioch, Reed, Swarthmore, and San Francisco State colleges, and less intensively at St. Olaf, the university of the Pacific, the University of Portland, and the University of California at Berkeley. On such studies will depend our greater ability to guide students in the choice of institutions, fields of study, and vocational careers.[15]

CHARACTERIZING COLLEGE ENVIRONMENTS

An important phase of the Center's study of student development is an analysis of the characteristics of the colleges themselves as social institutions and of the impact of college character on students of varying characteristics. The systematic description and measurement of college environments has only begun. If a better pairing of students and institutions is to be attained,

[15] C. E. Bidwell (ed.), *The American College and Student Personality: A Survey of Research, Progress, and Problems* (report of a conference on research on college influences on personality under the auspices of the Committee on Personality Development in Youth of the Social Science Research Council, Andover, Massachusetts, March, 1959), Social Science Research Council, New York, 1960.

it will be necessary to make a full assessment not only of student characteristics and potentialities for development but also of the characteristics of college environments and of the way in which student and college characteristics interact. An important contribution to institutional analysis has been made by Dr. C. Robert Pace and Dr. G. G. Stern of Syracuse University. Pace writes: "The press of the environment, as the student sees it, defines what he must cope with and clarifies for him the direction his behavior must take if he is to find satisfaction and reward within the dominant culture of the college." [16] To get at the "press" or "presses" of an institution, Stern and Pace devised the College Characteristic Index. Students are asked to indicate whether each of the 300 statements in the Index is characteristic of the institution they are attending. From an analysis of students' responses in sixty diverse colleges and universities, Pace concluded that there are two major foci around which most differences among college environments rotate, one intellectual, the other social. Within these broad categories five types of environments may be found. The intellectual environment is of two sorts, humanistic or scientific. The dominant concern in the third type of environment is with practical activities rather than abstract ideas. The fourth type emphasizes human relations, group welfare, social responsibility, and the well-mannered and well-managed community. The fifth is described as a rebellion against an emphasis on group welfare and community values.

Pace has summarized the characteristics of these environments as follows: [17]

The first is predominantly humanistic, reflective, and sentient. College is an expanding intellectual experience, testing the limits of curiosity about new ideas, new sensations, new capacities, and self-understanding. The second,

[16] C. R. Pace, "Five Psychological Differences between College Environments," *College Board Review*, Spring, 1960, pp. 24–28.
[17] *Ibid.*

equally demanding and vigorous, is predominantly scientific and competitive, requiring a high degree of individual concentration for survival. The third is practical, applied, concerned with inter-personal and extra-personal status. In the pursuit of utilitarian goals, one's relationship to authority and the gaining of privileges and visible rewards are important. The fourth type of environment is strongly other-directed. There is a high level of concern for group welfare, friendships, organization, and social responsibility. The fifth type is aggressive and impulsive, in rebellion chiefly against the other-directed, highly socialized community.

Pace explored the relationship between these five kinds of college environments and summarized his findings as follows: [18]

> The variables which push toward intellectual expansion and achievement, whether humanistic or scientific, correlate positively among themselves and negatively with the practical status-oriented variables. The humanistic emphasis is unrelated to the group welfare emphasis and unrelated to rebelliousness. Apparently the strongly science-oriented environment is also characterized by non-conformity and independence. The status-oriented, practical environment has some positive relationship to rebellion but little or no relationship to group welfare. It is clearly anti-intellectual but not anti-knowledge. The college as a friendly, socializing, well-mannered environment is not anti-intellectual in general, but it is anti-scientific and competitive, and anti-rebellious.

SUITING STUDENTS TO ENVIRONMENTS

Pace pointed out that no one type of college may be expected to serve effectively all kinds of students. For example, the friendly,

[18] *Ibid.*

social, group welfare kind of college culture should be good
for future residents in suburbia and for the training of employees
and managers of businesses that stress human relations. Such an
environment, he observed, might be especially valuable for
women, since fellowship is an important virtue. He pointed out,
however, that in the modern world socialization is not enough;
it is important to ask what ends togetherness should serve. The
rebellious environment, on the other hand, merely reacts against
socialization without offering any positive direction. Pace goes
on to say: [19]

> The practical, status-oriented environment doubtless pro-
> vides needed skills for society's work; and for some it may
> offer practice in the struggle for room at the top. For most,
> it seems more likely to be a good influence in maintaining
> a *status quo* of ideas and human relations; and in this sense
> it can be called a containment environment. For the bright
> and adventurous, the intellectual-humanistic-scientific en-
> vironment is full of promise and excitement. It may be an-
> noyingly rebellious at times for the administrator, and it
> may not have much good neighborly spirit in it, but it is
> potentially creative. It offers the hope of an adolescent break-
> through toward new directions, new solutions, and new
> ways of life.

Preliminary studies of the congruence of student characteristics and college environments suggest that some students tend
to choose institutions which will support their needs and motivations. Students with serious academic motivation and a high
degree of intellectual independence may be expected to choose
a college in this image and presumably thrive in its atmosphere.
If, however, intellectually conventional, dependent, and rigid
students enter the same institution, they may leave it soon, finding

[19] *Ibid.*

it uncongenial and threatening. Should these students have attended a college which would satisfy their need for authority, constraint, and conformity? After exploring the relationships between student characteristics and college environments, Stern suggested that the optimum college environment for a particular student might be one which provided maximum stimulation toward change rather than maximum satisfaction and support or even minimum strain.[20]

Stern participated in studies which showed that academic performance can be predicted to a surprising degree by the congruence between student needs and college press. For example, students were given an instrument called An Inventory of Beliefs, which yields scores positively related to those on a well-known authoritarian scale. Students at one extreme on this inventory were said to be characterized by "depersonalized and codified social relationships, pervasive acceptance of authority as absolute, inhibition and denial of impulses, rigid orderliness and conformity in behavior." These were called the stereopaths. At the opposite extreme, students were said to exhibit "highly personalized and individualized social relationships, pervasive rejection of authority figures, spontaneous and acceptant impulse life, and nonconforming flexibility in behavior." These were said to be the nonstereopaths.

The attainment and persistence of the two extreme groups were studied in a college which put a premium on high academic achievement and which was predominantly concerned with the intellectual development of the students. Grades were based entirely on the results of comprehensive examinations which emphasized critical, evaluative, and constructive thinking rather than the reproduction of what had been presented or read.

[20] G. G. Stern, "Congruence and Dissonance in the Ecology of College Students," *Student Medicine*, vol. 8, no. 4, pp. 304–309, April, 1960.

Of the stereopaths, 30 per cent made a comparatively poor adjustment to the college as revealed by advisers' comments concerning emotional stability or erratic behavior; the percentage for the nonstereopaths was 15. Of the stereopaths, 23 per cent had been dropped or had withdrawn by the end of the first year, most of them by the end of the first semester; only 1 per cent of the other group had left in the same period. The stereopaths experienced particular difficulty in the humanities and the social sciences, in which the educational program emphasized abstract analysis and relativity of values rather than fixed standards. The relatively unsuccessful performance of the stereopaths was reflected in the fact that the scholastic and social environment of the institution in question was basically opposed to the rigidity, conventionality, dependence, and general orientation of the stereopathic student.[21]

Stereopaths can be changed, but special methods of instruction are necessary to make them less rigid, dependent, and intellectually conventional.[22] Optimum development of students who differ in such fundamental elements of social, emotional, and intellectual disposition as those under discussion depends on the selection or modification of college environments with their special sanctions and demands.

There is a further complication in analyzing college environments and in judging under what cultures students might develop most fully. Pace seems to be justified in describing the dominant characteristics of a total college environment, but most institutions, especially large complex universities, are not all of a piece. It is often possible to identify fairly well-defined subcultures in the whole. Among the small liberal arts colleges which the

[21] G. G. Stern, M. I. Stein, and B. S. Bloom, *Methods in Personality Assessment*, The Free Press, Glencoe, Ill., 1956.

[22] G. G. Stern, "Congruence and Dissonance in the Ecology of College Students," *Student Medicine*, vol. 8, no. 4, pp. 304–309, April, 1960.

Center is studying, one has what might be characterized as a narrow environment, that is, students cannot find many alternatives in this college. If they are uninterested in meeting the stiff intellectual demands of this community, there is little for them to do but withdraw or subordinate their other desires to the intellectual press of the college. The Center found that another college offers a number of alternatives: theoretically oriented students may respond to one aspect of the environment, while practically oriented students may find opportunities in engineering, business administration, and recreation. The number and variety of subcultures are, of course, even greater in a large university. Here a wide range of specializations is available among which most students can find a place congruent with their interests, abilities, and goals. Furthermore, a large institution may have a much more diverse student body than a smaller, highly selective one. Thus, a wide range of student cultures may be found. Students with intellectual, humanistic interests will find many avenues of expression, both curricular and extracurricular. And students with interest in science will find a full range of specializations available. There are professional curricula which satisfy practical interests, and there are fields in which social relationships are important to success, perhaps in the university and almost certainly in later careers. Some campuses, too, provide opportunities for student rebellion. In fact, these subcultures often lend color and excitement to the university community. Unfortunately, many universities also offer an environment for play, with their fraternities and sororities, their intercollegiate athletic programs, and other educationally and intellectually questionable features.

The ideal in a diversified system of higher education is to aid each student to find the institution, the curriculum, the student and faculty associations which will enable him to realize his potentialities most fully. But, as said before, our present stage of knowledge concerning the differences among students and differences within individuals, the requirements of the multitude of careers which are open to educated men, and the characteristics of college environments and college subcultures will not permit us to attain this pairing with any degree of precision. Research on student characteristics and on the nature of college environments and of the interaction of the two in student development during the college years has scarcely begun. But behavioral scientists are now attacking these problems, bringing to bear upon them the methodologies and concepts of many related disciplines. We may expect in the next decade to learn far more about ways to stimulate desirable change in college students. Then and only then will we be able to guide them into appropriate educational opportunities with any degree of confidence.

Until we understand students more fully and have clearer ideas about the college experiences which will be most fruitful for them, many will make false starts and find it necessary to change directions. In some instances this may mean changing from one curriculum to another in the same institution. In a functionally differentiated system of public higher education in which some fields and levels of specialization are assigned to particular institutions, change of direction may mean transferring from one institution to another. Within the present limits of our knowledge about the "fit" between students and institutions, it would be indefensible, even in a coordinated and differentiated system, to assign a student once and for all to a particular institution or a specific curriculum. The system must be flexible enough to enable each student to reach the highest level for which his aptitude and performance qualify him.

INDEX

Differentiation, in agriculture, 71–
    74
    attitudes toward, of faculty,
        63–64
    of parents, 63
    of students, 63
    in California, 79, 155–159
    in engineering, 56, 69–70
    in functions, 59, 101, 105,
        190
    constitutional definition
        undesirable, 154–155
    obstacles to, 63–64, 77–78
    within institutions, 40–41
Diversity (see Institutional diver-
    sity; Student characteristics)
Douglas, A. A., 67
Duplication, consequences of, 136
    unnecessary, 63–64

Eddy, E. D., 95, 96
Educational Policies Commission,
    9
Educational Testing Service, 69
Edwards Personal Preference
    Schedule, 180
Eikenberry, D. H., 126
Elmo Roper Associates, 1
Engineering, 52
    differential programs in, 69
    differentiation in tasks, 69–70,
        181
Engineering Council for Profes-
    sional Development, 69
England, 48, 162, 165
    Education Act of 1944, 171

England, technical education, 48–
    50
    coordination in, 162–165
    White Paper on, 49
    university coordination, 165–
        169
    University Grants Commit-
        tee, 162
Enrollment, 9, 17
    college attendance and father's
        occupation, 29–30
    large increases expected, 9–10
    society's influence on, 17
    and toleration for restric-
        tions, 17
Excellence, institutional, stand-
    ards of, 80–82
Extension centers, 131
    versus junior colleges, 132–134

Farwell, E. D., 74
Flexibility, educational, 174–179,
    190
Florida, 124
    junior college development,
        124–125
Folwell, William Watts, 91, 111
Freedman, M. B., 182
Fund for the Advancement of
    Education, 178, 179
Funkenstein, D. H., 36

Gardner, John, 47, 81
Gee, H. H., 25, 181

Date Due